The Externalisation of Asylum Procedures

European University Studies
Europäische Hochschulschriften
Publications Universitaires Européennes

Series XXXI
Political Science

Reihe XXXI Série XXXI
Politikwissenschaft
Sciences politiques

Vol./Bd. 540

PETER LANG
Frankfurt am Main · Berlin · Bern · Bruxelles · New York · Oxford · Wien

Elisabeth Haun

The Externalisation of Asylum Procedures

An Adequate EU Refugee Burden Sharing System?

PETER LANG
Europäischer Verlag der Wissenschaften

Bibliographic Information published by the Deutsche Nationalbibliothek
The Deutsche Nationalbibliothek lists this publication in the Deutsche Nationalbibliografie; detailed bibliographic data is available in the internet at <http://www.d-nb.de>.

ISSN 0721-3654
ISBN-10: 3-631-56277-2
ISBN-13: 978-3-631-56277-2

Printed in Germany 1 2 3 4 5 7

www.peterlang.de

Foreword

By Prof. Dr. Heinrich Neisser

A broad majority of European Union (EU) citizens is affected by the incredibly high frequency of media reports about refugees drowning at the Mediterranean, but also about refugees arriving at the European coast. It is obvious that a solution needs to be found. In this context, in 2003, Tony Blair proposed the establishment of EU reception camps including the capacity of conducting asylum procedures in North African states. Otto Schily reproduced the idea a year later. The potential solution astonishes due to the simplicity of its argumentation: refugees will not drown at sea anymore if they do not need to come to the EU to seek asylum. It might be this simplicity that is attractive to many people. It is this simplicity that asks for substantiated examination.

Elisabeth Haun succeeded in producing a substantiated examination by identifying the strengths and weaknesses of the proposals concerning the externalisation of asylum procedures. The potential consequences of the idea are comprehensively examined from a legal, a humanitarian, a political and an economic point of view. Additionally, a wide range of circulating opinions are captured and the elaboration of the proposals is evaluated by using a project evaluation frame. Finally, the incorporation of the externalisation debate into the burden sharing debate reveals the broader connections of the subject in question.

The comprehensive approach of the author enables the reader to form an opinion that considers a high number of concerned aspects.The incorporation of a variety of perspectives forms the basis of the potency of this work. Additionally, the research subject is of high importance and topicality within the political agenda of the European Union. That motivated among others my supervision decision. Elisabeth Haun wrote an outstanding publication. Even if it was already handed in in November 2005, the information did not forfeit any of its relevance.

Innsbruck, November 2006
Heinrich Neisser

Foreword - Update

The publication in hand was written as a diploma thesis supervised by Prof. Dr. Heinrich Neisser at the Leopold-Franzens-University in Innsbruck, Austria. The faculties concerned are both political science and economy. Since its publication at university dates from November 2005, this foreword aims at an update to maintain its topicality. Even if the externalisation of asylum procedures has hardly appeared on the European Union's political agenda since then, details updating the work are required and each chapter is summarised in turn.

Chapter two treats the burden-sharing debate, its history, reasons and instruments. Statistical data has obviously changed, although the tendency towards declining numbers of refugees within the European Union (EU) persists. To guarantee topicality for future readers, it seems to be more expedient to state homepages where up-to-date material may be downloaded at any time. The statistical area of the UNHCR[1] offers both statistical yearbooks as well as reports on quarterly asylum trends.
In its Communication on Policy priorities in the fight against illegal immigration of third-country nationals in July 2006, the Commission focuses on the importance of burden sharing within the EU: "Solidarity, mutual trust and shared responsibility between Member States is a key requirement in an area without internal borders, which poses a particular burden with respect to pressure from illegal immigration on Member States who control an external border."[2] Referring to this Communication, the Finnish presidency launched the idea of a financial burden sharing mechanism based on the registration of migrants in September 2006. Each registration implies the member state's right to financial support for reception, maintaining and possible return, but also the responsibility for the person in question.[3]

Several ideas for externalised asylum procedures are presented in Chapter three. The current state - chapter (3.1.2) on the level of the EU foresees studies on joint processing of asylum applications within as well as outside the EU territory. Scheduled publication for these studies was

[1] http://www.unhcr.org/statistics
[2] COM(2006) 402 final, p.3
[3] "Migration management; extended european solidarity in immigration, border control and asylum policies", http://www.eu2006.fi/news_and_documents/other_documents/vko36/en_GB/1157615544264/_files/75865498810319023/default/extended_solidarity_EN.pdf

2006. Further research[4] revealed that the studies will not be finished by 2006, but are intended to be conducted in 2007.
In the meantime, a variety of subject-related papers were published by the Commission of the EU, for instance the Policy Plan on Legal Migration in December 2005[5] and the proposal for a regulation establishing Rapid Border Intervention Teams[6] in July 2006. Moreover, a council directive on minimum standards on procedures in Member States for granting and withdrawing refugee status[7] was adopted in December 2005. These papers correspond indirectly to the externalisation of asylum procedures since they all treat migration issues. Nevertheless, papers directly affecting the externalisation debate are not intended until results of the above-mentioned studies are available. Or, as the European Commission puts it in a Communication from the 3rd of June: "The various legal, financial and practical questions surrounding the proposed reshaping of asylum procedures, proposed by the UK, in particular in relation to the notion of transit processing centres, need to be researched and answered before taking any further position."[8] For this reason, the topicality of this work does not suffer from the delay of one year.

Finally, the analysis in chapter four does not forfeit its relevance since it is based on proposals made in the years 2003 and 2004 that have not been changed. Updated information is not required.

For further information on new tendencies within the EU at any given time, I highly recommend either contacting the agency of the European Commission in Vienna[9] or the European telephone (Europatelefon) within the Austrian Federal Chancellery[10].

Innsbruck, November 2006
Elisabeth Haun

---

[4] Information obtained by Jean-Jacques Nuss from the department A5 (information and communication) within the Commission of the European Union, forwarded by Bernard Kuhr, representant of the European Commission in Vienne on the 27th of October 2006.
[5] COM(2005) 669 final
[6] COM(2006) 401 final
[7] Council directive 2005/85/EC
[8] COM(2003) 315 final, p.6-7
[9] http://ec.europa.eu/austria/
[10] http://www.europa.gv.at/

Table of Contents

1 Introduction

Research Impulse

In spring, when it becomes warmer, the travel season starts. Some take a trip to the sunny south to get a tan, but at the same time thousands of refugees head north trying to reach Europe with the aim of restarting their lives. The majority among them already have had a hard time on their way through Africa to reach a North African country. Then, being separated from Europe only by the Mediterranean, the dream of Europe seems to be incredibly near.

In spring, when it becomes warmer, newspapers report about refugees that have drowned in the Mediterranean because the overcrowded and old ships sink. Obviously, a variety of people are outraged by this, because nobody wants refugees to drown at sea. If then a solution for the problem of their drowning at sea is offered, I am happy, everybody is happy. In summer 2004, after a further refugee drama in the Mediterranean sea, Otto Schily, the German Home minister, proposed EU (European Union) reception camps in a North African state. The EU would invest into the externalisation of asylum procedures so that the refugees have the possibility to seek asylum in an EU member state without going there. At first sight, it seems promising. Without reflection, any type of solution is always welcome. Therefore, I was interested to know if a deeper investigation would reveal if this "solution" could be effective.

Problem

After World War II, the majority of the old EU Member States were incredibly inventive when it came to creating incentives for foreigners to come to their states. The reason for this was that they needed a working population. As the unemployment rate increased in the late 1960's and early 1970's, almost all over Europe borders were closed for traditional working migration. The remaining possibilities for immigrants to gain access to Europe were, most prominently, through very widely defined family reunification policies. As European policy makers recognized the ineffectiveness of these paths because of the overuse by all kinds of "family members", restrictions were added to reunification policies. As a consequence, economic migrants gradually emerged in the asylum channel as this became more or less the only opportunity to reach Europe.

The result is constantly increasing asylum application rates which are more and more perceived as a burden. Therefore an instrument to decrease the number of asylum applications needs to be found.

Structure and Aims

The escalating migration pressure in the late 1980's together with more conscious public opinion in the early 1990's catapulted asylum on top of the political agenda. Confronted by this increased attention, the differences in asylum policies in different nations became obvious. The burden of hosting asylum seekers, as it was more and more perceived, was very unequally distributed between several EU Member States. The situation in the other OECD countries was very similar. This poured into tensions between the most and the less concerned countries – the burden sharing debate was born. Chapter two will deal with the historical background of the burden-sharing debate, the existence of unequal distribution and the reasons for it (2.1). Furthermore, Chapter two explores a variety of burden-sharing instruments like policy harmonisation, quotas or market mechanisms. The first two instruments do not foresee physical transfer of asylum seekers. In contrast, market mechanism within the area of asylum would imply trade and, as a consequence, physical transfer of asylum seekers (2.2).

The EU is currently on the way to a Common European Asylum System. The discussions relating to it brought out the idea of extra-territorial processing for asylum seekers. Chapter three is devoted to the rise of the externalisation idea within the EU. The key role of this development befits the UK (United Kingdom) who, in Spring 2003, suggested an external solution. It included the installation of reception camps outside the EU, for instance in the Ukraine, to where certain categories of spontaneous arrivals could be sent to have their claim processed. If granted asylum, the refugee status would open for them a way to Europe. If not, they would be sent back to their regions of origin (3.1). A UNHCR counterproposal followed, confirming central reception camps from where the refugees could be distributed. Contrary to the UK proposal, the UNHCR wanted such a camp to be at the borders, but inside the EU (3.2). A reaffirmation of the externalisation idea by Otto Schily, the German Home minister, preoccupied the media in 2004. He suggested the installation of reception camps in Northern African countries (3.3).
However, even if these proposals seem to be new approaches, the externalisation idea is neither new – similar proposals already existed in the 1980's and 1990's – nor a European speciality. The United States

have experiences with extra-territorial processing at Guantanamo Bay in the mid 1990's, while Australia's South Pacific Solution is sending asylum seekers to non-Australian territory where their applications have been processed since 2001 (3.4).
As a result, Chapter two and Chapter three are synthesised so that the instrument of extra-territorial processing is included in the burden-sharing debate. It may be interpreted as a burden-sharing instrument that incorporates a "trade" component into the asylum field. Physical transfer would then be the result (3.5).

The aim of this paper is to analyse extra-territorial processing. As mentioned above, the idea of this paper developed in the context of Otto Schily's suggested solution to the refugee drowning in the Mediterranean Sea. He argued that the installation of EU reception camps in a North African state would contribute to the reduction of deaths and injuries on refugees' journeys to the EU.

Further research also showed that the real problem for the EU is the high number of asylum applications. It was therefore recognised that on the way to creating a Common EU asylum system, more efficiency would be necessary. This was evident from several communication papers (European Commission) and presidency conclusions (European Council). The UK proposal of externalised EU reception camps also aims at more efficiency. The efficiency aim may therefore be assumed to be an additional motivation for an external solution. If there are other forces behind the externalisation idea than the humanitarian ones, it is highly important to examine the potential consequences so that we know to which kind of instruments it refers. Therefore, the question of this paper asks if the externalisation of asylum procedures would be an adequate EU refugee burden sharing system. Chapter four will try to answer this question.

But before that we need to define what "adequate" stands for. A measure is adequate if it is compatible with international law and principles; if it is acceptable from a humanitarian point of view; if it is politically feasible; and if it reaches the envisaged aims. Chapter four is based on three strands. First (4.1), it is outlined who (politicians, political parties, a variety of organisations) actually estimate the externalisation idea to be adequate or not. The voices rejecting this solution agree on its incompatibility with international law. Second (4.2), the "adequacy" of externalisation itself shall be examined from a legal, a humanitarian and a political point of view. An external solution is absolutely inadequate from the first two perspectives, but may be highly useful on a political level. Third (4.3), the examination will be extended by looking at the "adequacy" of externalisation as a burden sharing mechanism. The question will be asked: Does it contribute to reaching the aim of more efficiency or the aim of more equity? It will be shown that externalisation is – under certain circumstances – an instrument that leads to a more efficient burden sharing.

Method

Chapter two and three are devoted to explaining the circumstances in which an external solution is born and to present the different proposals concerning asylum. Therefore, this part of the work is purely descriptive. Due to the current importance of this subject, the sources used are mainly studies, communication papers, newspaper articles, and press releases.

In contrast, Chapter four is the analytical part of the paper. Chapter 4.1 contains an analysis of newspaper articles and communication papers of organisations. This analysis aims to describe the existing opinions about extra-territorial processing.

The analysis of documents in Chapter 4.2 uses a content analytical scheme of categories. First of all, a variety of documents were studied to get a general idea of externalisation. In a second step, based on the first lecture, relevant categories were determined inductively so that the external solution may be evaluated more easily. Through defining the categories, questions arose which I attempted to answer. Third, an analysis frame was established by using the structure of the evaluation scheme of Secours Catholique, a French relief organisation. But since a framework does not meet up with all the criteria necessary to analyse the outsourcing of asylum, this frame has been revised and extended by the categories determined inductively. Therefore, it was possible to include legal and political criteria to be able to determine the adequacy of externalised reception camps.

Finally, to evaluate the adequacy of a measure, it seems highly important to investigate the extend to which the envisaged aims are reached. These are in the case of burden sharing instruments more equity or more efficiency. Therefore, Chapter 4.3 examines if externalisation is an instrument aimed at reaching more efficiency or more equity. This part of the paper is based on an economic qualitative analysis scheme created by Joseph E. Stiglitz and Bruno Schönfelder (1989) that heads towards the evaluation of public expenditure. It asks if there is a necessity for state intervention (in our case the EU). If this is the case, the analysis may continue with the efficiency and equity consequences of the external solution. Finally, the frame foresees the examination of the political decision-making process. This economic qualitative analysis scheme is especially useful in our area of examination because it deals with the equity-efficiency conflict. Furthermore, it must be noted that the externalisation proposals emphasised the efficiency aspect. Therefore, this part of the work concentrates on examining the effectiveness of the system to reach more efficiency. Alexander Betts (2005) claims for the investigation of efficiency to use a variety of fixings (how to define the cost term, which type of good, who shall profit, and which efficiency concept is applied). These fixings are done on the pattern proposed by Alexander Betts.

Defining some technical terms

Throughout the paper, asylum seekers are associated with the idea of a ***burden*** because this is done in the majority of the literature analysed. It must be noted that this term does not reflect the opinion of the author.

Furthermore, a variety of expressions stand for ***externalisation***. When terms like extra-territorial processing, the external solution, externalised and external EU reception camps are used, the same idea of externalisation is meant.

Finally, the term refugee might cause some confusion. In this work, ***refugee*** stands for a person that seeks protection. Synonymously, the term asylum seeker is used. When talking about a person who finally was granted the refugee status, it is explicitly indicated by employing expressions like recognised refugee or a person granted asylum.

2 The burden-sharing debate

2.1 Why burden sharing?

Before discussing the historical background of the burden-sharing debate and the reasons for the necessity of sharing a certain burden, the term "burden-sharing" shall be briefly explained. It is used in the occurrence of problems that do not refer to a certain nation state, but concern a variety of states. In the context of environment such a burden would for example be emissions that naturally do not respect national borders. To successfully reduce them, the concerned states would need to cooperate. Sharing the burden would signify that each concerned state contributes to the emissions reduction. In the same sense, the term of "burden-sharing" is frequently used in literature on asylum. Each state will contribute to the institution of asylum so that the burden of asylum may be shared.

2.1.1 Historical outline of migration movements and the burden-sharing debate

Fleeing people have always existed, a refugee status has not. It was only in the 17th century that the first refugees, the Huguenots leaving France, were recognised. Nevertheless, no refugee policy was established, each nation reacted with its own ad hoc approach to the problem. A significant change was introduced in the beginning of the 20th century, a period that is characterised by strongly increasing migration on a global scale. The Russian Revolution produced more than a million refugees between 1917 and 1921. As a response to the resulting mass migration, "The League of Nations High Commissioner for Refugees" was founded in 1921. But only 25 years later it was dissolved after World War II, when it was exposed to the incredible number of 30 million people who were not able to return home (Barnett 2002: 1-5). It then followed that the International Refugee Organisation (IRO) and with it the first burden-sharing mechanism was established. The majority of the uprooted people were successfully distributed among the USA, Canada, Australia, Western European Countries and Latin America. Even if it seemed to work relatively well, there was another side to the system since only "the most eligible had been picked" over a shorter period of time. The "hard core" of old and injured people in contrast needed to stay in camps. These people could be described as the losers of the instrument (Suhrke 1998: 404). However, a very important step in the development of a global refugee system was taken in 1951 when the United Nations High Commission for Refugees (UNHCR) was established and the Geneva Refugee Convention was signed. The refugee system is still based on the Refugee Convention and the UNHCR, even if the latter can be more flexible in taking steps today than initially (Barnett 2002: 6-7).

In the post-war era, the majority of the old EU (European Union) Member States were incredibly inventive concerning creating incentives for foreigners to come to their states. The main reasons were the shortage of labour forces and the fight against communism. For ideological reasons, countries of the so-called Western world were eager to receive refugees fleeing communism to "demonstrate the moral bankruptcy of" that system. This was especially true after the Hungarian revolt in 1956 and the "Prague Spring" in 1968. Heading towards the end of the Cold War, the ideological incentive to open the borders gradually disappeared. The economic incentive due to the post-war boom had already vanished two decades earlier. As the unemployment rate increased in the late 1960's and early 1970's due to the economic recession, almost all over Europe, borders were closed for the previously accepted migration of workers (Gibney 2004: 3). The remaining possibilities to immigrate were, most prominently, very widely defined family reunification policies. As European policy makers recognized the ineffectiveness of these paths because of the overuse by all kinds of "family members", restrictions were added to reunification policies (Gibney 2004: 14).

As a consequence, economic migrants gradually emerged in the asylum channel as this became more or less the only opportunity to reach Europe, hence to belong to the right side in a world of "uneven distribution of security and welfare across states" (Gibney 2004: 5). The result was an increase in asylum application rates. The escalating migration pressure in the late 1980's together with a more conscious public opinion in the early 1990's catapulted asylum to the top of the political agenda. Confronted by this issue coming more into the public eye, the differences in national asylum policies became obvious. The burden of taking asylum seekers, as it was more and more perceived, was very unequally distributed between several EU Member States. Globally, the situation was and still is even more disparate. "Even the desperately impoverished African states of Malawi, Burundi, Congo and Sudan share over a million refugees among them, many more than most liberal democratic states" (Gibney 2004: 4). This poured into tensions between the most and the less concerned countries – the burden sharing debate was born. "Burden-sharing instead of burden-shifting" as a goal still preoccupies the international community, academics, and policy makers. This objective describes the reality of how the burden is shared among nation states. Naturally, not every state invests voluntarily in the asylum system. In contrast, they try to transfer the burden to other states that for example have less political power. However, to reach the aim of burden-sharing instead of burden-shifting, a variety of burden-sharing mechanisms were developed on a theoretical level and will be presented in Chapter 2.2.

EU burden-sharing debate since the 1990's

The war in former Yugoslavia from 1991 to 1995 caused mass refugee influxes to Western European Countries whose reactions were particularly restrictive. The result: only a small number of refugees were resettled without any co-ordinated co-operation among the other European States. Furthermore, visa policy was used to close the borders. However, some 600,000 refugees were able to enter the EU before those visa restrictions came into force. Most concerned were Sweden, Austria, Germany and Switzerland. Not surprisingly, those countries were the driving forces in the European burden-sharing debate at that time. Austria and Sweden, not EU Members by then, brought in a proposal in November 1993 simply aiming at improving equity in distribution. The strong French and British opposition resulted in further discussions; the Austrian-Swedish proposal was not adopted. The main argumentation was based on the French and British peace-keeping missions in Yugoslavia which needed to be counted against the in-country refugee reception. Only then could a comprehensive equity be reached. The European Commission communication and European Parliament resolutions followed. Finally, in September 1995, the "Resolution on Burden-Sharing with Regard to the Admission and Residence of Displaced Persons on a Temporary Basis" was adopted. It represented a watered-down version of a draft resolution prepared by Germany a year before that headed towards a quota-based burden-sharing (See 2.2). However, the 1995 resolution laid down that, in case of a refugee emergency, harmonised reception should lead to more equitable burden sharing. As demanded by France and the UK, peace-keeping contributions may be counted as part of the burden. This approach has been extended by a proposal made by the European Commission in 1997 that envisaged harmonised action on a temporary basis only after collective decision-making. Once again, the key role in the burden-sharing mechanism is played by policy harmonisation (Suhrke 1998: 406-412). Finally, some examples of EU legislation heading towards harmonisation of asylum policy shall be listed:
1995: Resolution on Minimum Guarantees for Asylum Procedures (Council Resolution)
1999: Aim of a Common European Asylum Policy (in the Treaty of Amsterdam)

2002: Agreement on a common definition of the refugee status (Justice and Home Affairs Council, Brussels)
2003: Directive on common reception conditions (European Commission) (Thielemann 2005: 15)

2.1.2 Unequal distribution of asylum seekers – statistics

The majority of the information used in this chapter was found in the UNHCR report on "Asylum Levels and Trends in Industrialized Countries: An Overview of asylum applications lodged in Europe and Non-European Industrialized Countries in 2004" published on the 1st March 2005. It was the most up-to-date and largest collection of data to be found. The statistics count one application per country as one asylum seeker. If a second application in one country is lodged, it is not counted. Nevertheless, it is very likely that the number of asylum seekers is overestimated since an asylum seeker may be counted twice as he/she lodges an application in two different countries (UNHCR 2005: 2).
The presentation of the data in turn emphasises two aspects. On the one hand, the overall drop of asylum applications in the 50 industrialised countries is an empirical evidence for burden-shifting from richer to poorer countries. Although the migration pressure is increasing, the number of applications is decreasing. Thus, the aim of burden-sharing instead of burden-shifting remains, up to now, very theoretical. The unequal distribution of asylum seekers on an international level is inevitable, especially because of the fact that the majority of the richer countries were strongly restricting its asylum policy. But also within these 50 industrialised countries, the acceptance of asylum claims is very unequally distributed as it is presented further down.

Overall drop in the number of applications

The fact that the number of asylum applications strongly decreased in the 50 examined industrialised countries is a real indication of the world wide trends and interesting for the following asylum debate which focuses on the European desire to externalise asylum procedures.

It is obvious that from 2001 to 2004, the number of asylum seekers fell in Europe, the United States, Canada, Australia and New Zealand. The enlarged EU registers a decline of 36 per cent in these three years, while the new EU Member States only register minus 12 per cent.

Concerning the non EU States, the numbers are even more significant. The United States and Canada recorded a decline of 48 per cent from 2001 to 2004, while in Australia and in New Zealand it fell by 74 per cent. The latter result is certainly connected to Australian's restrictive asylum policy, called the South-Pacific Solution, which sends shipwrecked asylum seekers to reception camps in the South-Pacific region, such as, to Nauru or Papua New Guinea (3.4.1).

If we take a closer look at the development from 2003 to 2004, it followed the current trend as is shown in the decline in the number of applications by 21 per cent for the 15 "old" EU Member States, by 26 per cent for North America and by 28 per cent for Australia and New Zealand. Only the 10 "new" European Union Member States registered a modest increase of 4 per cent (UNHCR 2005: 3-4). There might be two reasons for this. First, they became more attractive because of their EU membership. Second, the Dublin convention[11] logically leads to a higher number of applications in the Border States because the EU-15 successfully shifted burden to the new members.

Unequal distribution within the industrialized countries

Referring to absolute numbers, the top asylum receiving countries from 2000 to 2004 were the USA, followed by the UK and Germany. Talking about burden, absolute numbers do not give enough information. Therefore, the number of applications per 1000 inhabitants is examined in turn and changes the picture. The new rank from 2000 to 2004: Cyprus with 22.2 applications per 1000 inhabitants, Austria with 17.9 and Norway with 14.8. The number-one country in absolute numbers, the USA, falls back on position 25 with 1.4 claims per 1000 inhabitants, the UK on rank 14 (6.7 applications per 1000 inhabitants) and Germany at rank 19 (3.9). While in the USA, 1000 inhabitants need to pay for 1.4 asylum seekers, 1000 Cypriotes are responsible for 22.2. There is empirical evidence which might explain the unevenness in the distribution, but before we try to answer this question, further information concerning the unequal distribution of asylum applications will be presented.

---

[11] Asylum seekers must lodge their application for asylum in the first EU country in which they arrive and may be returned to it if it can be shown that they have either passed through it or made an application for asylum in it. Obviously, Member States at the border of the EU are very much concerned by the Dublin Convention. Countries like Germany are the winners of such a system. Available at: http://www.irishrefugeecouncil.ie/factsheets/dublinconvention4.html [accessed 11 May 2005].

In May 2005, Mathias Czaika (Institute for Economic Research, University of Freiburg, Germany) presented a Refugee Burden Index to measure the degree of over-burden. A detailed explication of the Index would go too far here. However, it is based on the Refugee Capacity Index and on the Refugee Gap. The first contains an economic element (income per capita), an acceptance element dependent on population density, and a political-institutional element apt to manage societal stability (quality of democratic institutions). The latter describes the gap between the normative and the real refugee population in a country (Czaika 2005: 6-11). Out of this information, this paper draws the degree of burden for 174 countries. The results: the globally 20 most burdened countries may be divided in 16 African countries, two European countries (Armenia and Serbia & Montenegro), Iran and Pakistan. Interestingly, the refugee population of these is very homogeneous. In contrary to that, the refugee population in Western European countries is highly heterogeneous. The most burdened countries within the EU are Sweden (globally rank 29), the Netherlands (globally rank 31) and Denmark (globally rank 32). To summarise some specific findings of the global unevenness, Africa and Caswaname are strongly over-burdened, Asia-Pacific and the Americas are under-burdened, while Europe is slightly under-burdened. Even if the outcome does not correspond to the abovementioned rank in detail, the tendency is the same. Globally, the asylum burden is very unequally distributed weighing on the poorest countries in the world. Regarding the EU, the same picture occurs. The poorer countries like Armenia and Serbia & Montenegro need to carry a larger burden than richer countries (Czaika 2005:14-16).

2.1.3 The reasons for unequal distribution

This work classifies two main reasons for unequal distribution of the "asylum burden" exercising influence on either the migration decision of the asylum seeker or on the perception decision of the host country's population.

As Thielemann (2003) impressively shows, certain pull factors may have a large impact on the attractiveness of a potential host country to the asylum seeker. Thus, different intensity in the existence of pull factors may explain the asylum seeker's decision for a certain country finally leading to unequal distribution. The second reason concerns a very subjective perception. Especially due to presentation in media and by politicians, public opinion distinguishes between various degrees of costs and benefits of asylum seekers. Dependant on the perceived net costs, hence costs minus benefits, asylum seekers will be classified by the public opinion as "burden" or as enrichment. This categorisation does not only refer to different perspectives – first, of the asylum seeker, second, of the host country's population – but also different burden definitions. While in the first case, asylum burden is simply seen as a share of asylum seekers in the total population, the second part defines it as the connected costs and benefits arising from asylum seekers.

2.1.3.1 Differences in pull factors

Eiko Thielemann (2003: 18-19) wrote an excellent work on the impact of pull factors by empirically testing a hypothesis. He used aggregated data for 20 OECD-countries covering the time period from 1985 to 1999. The data was provided by UNHCR, OECD and the U.S. Committee for Refugees. His quantitative analysis is based on one dependent variable and some explanatory variables. The latter describe causes that influence the dependent variable. As a consequence, changes in explanatory variables lead to changes in the dependent variable which need to be measured to see the relative impact of different causes. The dependent variable contains two aspects. It describes the number of asylum applications in one country in one year relative to its population and relates it to the relative number of asylum applications in the totality of the 20 OECD countries. It is more useful to examine the impact of the pull factors on relative than absolute values since the latter would give a distorted image in a world of countries with very different population sizes. The pull factors, here the independent variables, will be presented in turn.

Historical ties / networks

Historical ties subsist between a country and its colony, networks between a community containing a certain immigration population and their relatives, friends, etc. in their home countries. Let's have a look at the example of Pakistanis and Bangladeshis in the United Kingdom (UK).

Their education, their language and their culture was very much influenced by their former colonial power which resulted in easier integration in the UK. That was an attractive factor for them as the large number of Pakistanis and Bangladeshis in the UK shows. The members of their communities have contact with their relatives and friends in their home countries. If one of them needs to seek asylum somewhere, it is very likely that he or she uses the existing network in an envisaged host country. Obviously, it is easier to go somewhere if information is provided and if a warm welcome, at least within the special community, is ensured (Thielemann 2003: 14-15). The hypothesis: a large stock of immigrants of a certain nation will positively influence the number of asylum applications. It is calculated by looking at the change in the number of asylum seekers from the top five countries of origin between period t-1 and t (Thielemann 2003: 20).

The economic factor

It is obvious that asylum seekers are less influenced by economic factors than the so-called "economic migrants", because their main reason to emigrate is persecution. But, as soon the decision to leave is made, economic factors may effect the choice of a certain host country. Thus, it explains why asylum seekers try to gain asylum more frequently in some countries more than in others. It has something to do with the possibilities of income maximisation and risk minimisation (Thielemann 2003: 13-14). The first is measured by looking at the GDP (Gross domestic product), the latter by the unemployment rate. The hypothesis: the relative number of asylum applications in a country will be positively correlated with its GDP, and negatively with its unemployment rate (Thielemann 2003: 19).

The geographic factor

Even if geographic proximity may be less important because of technological developments, facilitating longer journeys, it is assumed that they still have an impact on the relative burden. Especially by recognising that asylum seekers do not have the necessary finances at their disposal to undertake long-distance travel (Thielemann 2003: 16), a positive correlation of geographic proximity with the dependant variable is assumed. To examine this, the average distance between the capitals of the top five countries of origin of each year to the capital of the destination country is measured (Thielemann 2003: 20).

The liberalness factor

It could be assumed that information about a country like high human rights standards, warm reception of asylum seekers, integration efforts and liberal naturalisation tradition will positively influence the number of asylum seekers in their decision to come to a certain country (Thielemann

2003: 16). The factor of liberalness is in Thieleman's work determined by the share of overseas development aid in the GDP (Thielemann 2003: 20).

The deterrence factor

It could be assumed that deterrent asylum policy will decrease the number of asylum applications in a country. Deterrent policy might aim at restrictions in access control, determination procedures and integration (Thielemann 2003: 17) resulting in a certain "deterrence index" between 0 (least deterrent) and 5 (most deterrent). It contains five elements – safe third country provision, above-average rejection rates, limited movement possibilities, voucher system, and the prohibition to work – each of which is weighted with 0 if non existent and 1 if existent. Then, the numbers of a particular year in a particular country are added and form the deterrence index for the relevant country in the relevant year (Thielemann 2003: 20-23).

The outcome of the quantitative analysis[12]

Almost all of the hypotheses may be verified except the one concerning the geographic factor. It may be argued that being a victim of persecution, an asylum seeker wants to be far away from the threat. But all the other correlations were confirmed. In other words, it is empirically proven that the unemployment rate and deterrent policies put off asylum seekers, whereas historical ties/networks, the GDP and the overseas development aid payments attract them. However, the influence of the GDP remains small, while the development aid payments and the deterrence index are already having a larger impact. The significant factors in the latter are only two out of five elements, namely the prohibition to work and the above-average rejection rate. The most significant pull factors are a low unemployment rate and a large stock of foreigners belonging to a certain community, hence existing historical ties and networks (Thielemann 2003: 25-30).

---

[12] The analysis was realised by using pooled time series cross section which is a popular tool to analyse matters that concern several cross-sections (here 20 OECD countries) and several time periods (here the years between 1985 and 1999).

They show us that the most important reasons for unequal distribution are differences in the employment possibilities (prohibition to work, unemployment rate) and the number of foreigners belonging to the same group already being in a country. In my opinion and estimating it to be of high importance, these two reasons include a fairness factor. In other words, it means that those countries with high unemployment rates would be sought less by asylum seekers. Hence, the asylum burden defined as the ratio between the number of asylum seekers and the population would be less. An analogous argumentation might be put forward for the second highly significant pull factor. Similar cultural, educational and language background like in the case of the Pakistanis and Bangladeshis in the UK might strongly facilitate integration. It is certainly very positive if asylum seekers head towards countries where they are more easily integrated than in others. However, this fact cannot be over-interpreted since the impact of the other pull factors, although less strong are still existent, may distort the "fairness-advantage". Moreover it must be noted that, within a burden-sharing debate based on a burden defined as the relative number of asylum applications, such differences would contribute to even more unequal distribution. But the term burden might be used differently as it will be shown in the following case.

2.1.3.2 Differences in net marginal perceived costs

The population does not necessarily see the number of asylum seekers as the most important issue, but the connected consequences in terms of costs and benefits. Very often, the burden is only defined as the financial costs caused by asylum seekers, hence the direct payments for processing their claims, and the satisfaction of their needs in everyday life.
Before focusing the costs, the term "net marginal perceived costs" needs to be explained. Marginal costs in the asylum field describe the costs that arise if one additional asylum seeker arrives in the country. Net costs are defined as costs minus benefits. Hence, net marginal costs are the additional costs of one asylum seeker minus the benefits of the same one. The word "perceived" indicates that the costs can hardly be expressed in monetary terms, but largely depend on very subjective attitudes. The intensity of the costs will depend on public perception. That is the basis for the extension of the cost notion, including political and social ones. Social costs arise when the population sees asylum seekers as a burden, because they are seen as criminals and job robbers. It is very evident that the negative impression of asylum seekers is more common as it was in

earlier times. Such attitudes, again, may be reduced to the atmosphere towards foreigners created by politicians and especially by the media. In short, the worse the image of asylum seekers, the higher the perception of the connected costs. The political costs may be described as the pressure that the population may exercise on politicians and on the decision making process. In recent years, asylum became one of the major issues for the majority of governments. Assuming that the average voter is the centre of attention, it is his or her definition of perceived net costs that influences the restrictiveness of the asylum policy (Betts 2003: 12-15).

As mentioned above, the degree of liberalness or deterrence influences the attraction of a particular country for asylum seekers, thus the number of applications and the connected burden. As a result, differences in the perception of the net marginal costs of an additional asylum seeker influence the asylum burden. For instance, countries like the UK have very large net marginal perceived costs and less liberal asylum policies, while the more tolerant attitude and less net marginal perceived costs in Sweden result in more generous policies. That may be one reason why the distribution of asylum seekers in numbers is unequal. As a consequence, the burden as it is defined above varies among the states. Including the net marginal perceived costs could lead to a more equal burden distribution among the states even if it is unequal in numbers. Regarding that burden-sharing aims at better protection and assistance for a refugee (Suhrke 1998:398), it would be, in my opinion, highly preferential to distribute more asylum seekers to those countries where they are confronted with less racism or at least less racial and cultural difference from their own culture, while the less tolerant countries shall be concerned with fewer asylum seekers. Such a distribution should lead to better circumstances for asylum seekers and consequently makes sense. Obviously, if it was about laying down the number (or percentage) of applications for each country dependent on their net marginal perceived costs, it is very probable that the majority of countries would not reveal their real preferences.

In contrary to financial costs, it is very problematic to assess social and political costs. So even though it is problematic the following question remains: are there possibilities to assess those costs so that the real preferences may be revealed and, as a consequence, the protection of asylum seekers could be improved? This question leads us to the existing burden-sharing instruments.

2.2 Burden-sharing instruments – prerequisites and differences

2.2.1 Prerequisites for agreeing on burden-sharing

Experiences of burden-sharing in the past shall help to derive prerequisites for a burden-sharing agreement. Therefore, we might first ask why the burden-sharing after World War II worked relatively well. First of all, the sending and the receiver countries were culturally very close, thus, the integration costs were, compared to today, very low. Furthermore, the benefits from immigrants were certainly higher than today, since they satisfied the increased demand for labour due to the post-war boom. The perceived benefits were higher than the costs. Furthermore, each of those nations was to a greater or lesser extent involved in the war, hence in the refugee-building process which led to a certain responsibility. Finally, and extremely importantly, the burden-sharing was based on a single issue of emptying the European camps (Suhrke 1998: 404).

To summarise, how might a successful burden-sharing mechanism be reached? A possible answer: benefits exceeding costs, collective responsibility of nations involved in and an isolated historical event. These ingredients do not exist in this form today. It is impossible to speak of an isolated historical event, since refugees now occur in high numbers. As long as the causes for this still exist, refugees will continue to arrive. Therefore, reaching an agreement on a burden-sharing system would imply a process with a very indefinite time span. As a consequence, states will be more cautious to consent to such co-operations. Nevertheless, the post World War II experience shows that such a system might work more easily if the countries feel responsible and if they perceive a net benefit from the asylum seekers. The experiences after the end of the Vietnam War in 1975 confirm this recommendation. In the 1980's and 1990's, more than a million refugees were distributed in the western world.

As was the case after World War II, the responsibility sharing was based on a market mechanism. In other words, the industrialised states were allowed to "send officials to camps in the first asylum areas to select and process candidates for resettlement. (...) The market system of resettlement succeeded in creating reasonable compatibility between the needs of the receiving countries and the refugees". This practice was especially realised by the USA, Australia, Canada and France. Another reason why it worked comparatively well was the role of the USA which used all its power to push other countries towards responsibility sharing. Nevertheless, it was still the countries' decisions under which criteria they were willing to take in refugees (Suhrke 1998: 405-406).

The derived rule from both experiences: an agreement on burden-sharing will be reached more easily if benefit maximisation or cost minimisation, from the country's perspective, is possible. In other words, supposing that the protection of a certain number of refugees needs to be guaranteed, so as not to breach with the principle of international solidarity, it is always better for a country if that may be realised through the highest benefits or the lowest costs. As a result, the attitude towards refugees could be improved and lead to better reception, assistance and protection.

What influences the costs and benefits?

As mentioned in 2.1.3.2, costs also include social and political factors. These may, for instance, be decreased by opening its borders to a refugee population that better fits the host country. The latter will more likely choose people that speak the same language or have cultural similarities to decrease the perceived costs of integration. Decreasing the costs by changing the host country's attitude toward refugees should not be forgotten as a long term goal for politicians and media. Benefits arise for instance from employing refugees in sectors where there is a lack of labour. That implies that countries would need to select "their" refugees as Germany for example tried to by offering easier access to IT-specialists. But, from a humanitarian perspective, I estimate such selection processes as not desirable. The post-war experience shows that such a mechanism would lead to a hard core of old and sick people, really needing help, but not getting it. This group within the refugee population needs to be considered in the development of burden-sharing mechanisms.

Other benefits may occur by recognising the country's motivations. According to Thielemann (2005), these may be divided into norm-based and interest-based motivations. The first are related to the principle of international solidarity, but according to Thielemann these motivations should not be emphasised too much. "The hard bargaining that characterized the establishment of the European Refugee Fund and the inability to agree on a distribution key in the case of temporary protection measures (in the case of mass influx) tell us to be cautious in over-interpreting the frequent pledges of Community solidarity" (Thielemann 2005: 10-11).

There are three motivations that can be identified in the category of interest-based motivations. First of all, a country might be offered benefits from agreeing on burden-sharing by representing a certain kind of insurance in the case of mass influx. Such "refugee crisis insurance" might be reassuring for states as health insurances for individuals (Schuck 1997: 249-250).

Secondly, a country would agree, because it aims at objectives of a higher order. To state an example, a EU Member State would participate in a burden-sharing system within the EU to guarantee the continuation of their own integration into the Union even if the nation was not directly interested in the burden-sharing itself. Thirdly, co-operation might lead to more efficiency, hence offer the same protection at lower costs, and, as a consequence, the net benefit (benefits minus costs) would increase (Thielemann 2005: 12-14). The incorporation of the efficiency concept into the burden-sharing debate can be observed in the last few years and will be broadly discussed in 4.3 from an economic point of view.

2.2.2 Burden-sharing instruments

The aim of each burden sharing instrument is better protection and assistance for refugees. The logic behind this is that "states are more likely to offer protection if they can share the burden". For a long time, the burden-sharing debate aimed at a reduction of the inequities in distribution (Suhrke 1998: 398). In recent years, a more efficient burden-sharing mechanism was added as a second aim, as was, for instance, incorporated in the UK proposal (Betts 2005:4). In this context, a variety of burden-sharing models were introduced either aiming at a more equitable or later, a more efficient burden sharing system. Enhancing equity is in a loose form envisaged by policy harmonisation models and in a strict form by quota settings. To enhance efficiency, the quota-mechanism is enlarged by a trade-component to boost competition between the states.

Burden-sharing to enhance equity

The logic behind the harmonisation of rights model may be found in the abovementioned discussion of pull factors. An adaptation of the pull factors should lead to a more equitable burden, since the asylum seeker's decision may not be effected by those factors anymore. As we know, the policy pull factors may have an impact on the asylum seeker's decision. Thus, the model could work. But the most important pull factors will not be touched by policy harmonisation, hence they will still head towards unequal distribution. As mentioned in 2.1.1, the EU especially prefers the use of a policy harmonisation instrument. Being conscious about the weight of other pull factors, the EU decided that financial compensations would be granted to those receiving a disproportionate number of refugees. The policy harmonisation is used on a EU level and is not able to enhance equitable burden-sharing beyond the EU. Furthermore, it is, in contrary to the others, a weak instrument. Even if that is right, it has a decisive advantage: Refugees do not need to be physically transferred within a burden-sharing mechanism and consequently, they are less limited in their asylum decision (Suhrke 1998: 412).

A more direct form of burden-sharing could be achieved by quota-mechanisms. A kind of quota may be seen in the fiscal burden-sharing as it has been applied in the EU since the foundation of the European Refugee Fund (ERF, operating since 1 January 2000). Financial compensation payments are distributed among the Member States, containing a fixed and a proportional element. The first is an equal flat rate that does not effect burden-sharing. The latter depends on the absolute number of asylum seekers in a country not considering its population, GNP, size or other absorption capacities. That seems highly unfair since it is the relative value that counts. Therefore, it leads to a sub-optimal outcome. Furthermore, the ERF is still limited by its size, not being attributed a large impact on Member States' decision making in the asylum area (Thielemann 2005: 15-17).

Another example of a quota-based burden-sharing instrument is the German draft resolution in 1994 that proposed a certain kind of refugee insurance. Dependent on a quota, Member States would need to pay a certain sum. The quota would be defined by a country's GNP (Gross National Product), its population and its size and would have led to the following exemplary indicators: Germany 21, France 19, Italy 15, UK 14, Portugal 2, Denmark 1 and Luxembourg 0,1. In other words, for every protected refugee in Denmark, Germany needs to care for 21 of them. Or one refugee in Luxemburg would imply 190 in France, and so on. Finally, the refugees that exceed one country's quota may be offloaded to others. All of the quota elements in the German draft resolution disappeared when it was adopted in September 1995 (Suhrke 1998: 410). Such instruments as proposed by Germany would include physical transfer of refugees which adds a very new and delicate aspect to the burden-sharing debate.

Burden-sharing to enhance efficiency

The instruments fitting in this category head towards burden-sharing within a market mechanism. It may be seen as an enlargement of the quota-based mechanism including a trade component. Such ideas come very close to environmental economics proposing instruments such as the tradable emission certificates.

Peter H. Schuck (1997) theoretically introduced a "refugee crisis insurance" heading towards more efficiency by making it possible to trade in a market. Being conscious that such a venture would be tricky, he stated at the very beginning: "Although the proposal entails many problems, virtually all of those problems already exist, sometimes even to a greater degree, in the current system. For this reason, I urge the reader to keep the 'compared to what' question firmly in mind as she ponders these problems" (Schuck 1997: 250).
The proposal contains two major aspects: assigning quotas to all Member States and enabling trade in a market. What are the prerequisites for such a system? First of all, no country shall be obliged to participate in such a burden-sharing system. Consent is the aim. Second, the asylum seekers shall be distributed among many states, so that the burden per state may be minimised. Third, each state should not be burdened with more refugees than its absorption capacity allows (Schuck 1997: 276-277). Fourth, the quota mechanism needs to be limited. Countries that violate human rights must not participate. Countries at war, involved in natural disaster or under a minimum standard of living do not need to participate for a certain period of time (Schuck 1997: 281).

Before being able to calculate quotas, the overall burden needs to be defined "as the number of refugees who need to be offered protection" by an international agency. This definition obviously contains many difficulties. But Schuck argues that those difficulties already occur in the current system. As soon as the overall burden is defined, a quota for each state needs to be derived. What sort of criterion shall be considered in this process? Schuck suggests a "protection criterion" that means the capacity of a state to offer minimum safeguards to refugees including food, clothing, shelter and physical security. To measure it, national wealth shall be used since protective capacity strongly depends on the financial possibilities of a state and national wealth is quantifiable. Other criteria as for example the assimilative capacity are not only hard to quantify, but would also have a very strange impact. If the refugee burden depended on a country's success in assimilating foreigners, each country would have a large motivation to limit its assimilation efforts. The criteria of population and country size as proposed in the aforementioned German proposal do not need to be considered since they are expressed in a country's willingness to pay on the market. Singapore, for example, is a small and homogenous, but rich country. It would be ready to pay high compensation payments (Schuck 1997: 278-280). The Japanese solution in the burden-sharing process after the Vietnam War (See 2.2.1) confirms that countries would be ready to financially compensate other countries. Instead of opening its borders to refugees as the majority of the other industrialised countries did, Japan increased its payments (Suhrke 1998: 405).

To attribute the possibility of compensation payments instead of refugee protection to the nations, trade needs to be enabled. How should that work? For the purpose of trading, the quota will be divided into packages of obligation. Some or all of them may be transferred to one or more other states. Then, these states need to fulfil the quota. In the countermove, they receive some sort of compensation which might range from financial payments or credit to technical advice or political support (Schuck 1997: 283-284). Such market mechanisms would decrease the overall costs, because the refugee protection is done there where it is cheaper (Schuck 1997: 285). Thus, efficiency would be enhanced. It must be noted that Schuck did not use the efficiency term in this context, but this paper assumes that it to be appropriate. The reason: offering the same output (refugee protection) at lower costs (because it is moved from high-costs to low-costs states) is, from an economic point of view, productively efficient. Further details on that matter will be presented in 4.3. Finally, Schuck agrees on a variety of difficulties of the model, but asks "in view of both the deplorable status quo and the potential for human rights gains, can we afford not to try?" (Schuck 1997: 297).

All in all, it may be observed that the presentation of the different models followed the development from pure financial to financial and physical transfer. The purely financial instruments have either already been realised (ERF) or are close to realisation (Common EU Asylum Policy). The ones including physical transfer are, at least in the EU, not reality yet, but are being broadly discussed within the EU. One possible instrument is the externalisation of asylum procedures meaning the physical transfer to a country outside the EU. The connected proposals and ideas discussed within the EU are presented in turn.

3 Externalisation of asylum procedures – reception camp plans and realisations

3.1 The UK proposal – extra-territorial processing to put an end to the failures of current asylum systems

„The EU cannot carry on pursuing old solutions to the asylum problem that do not work, and do not tackle the root causes of migration flows and refugee displacement", said UK Home Secretary David Blunkett (UK Home Secretary 2003) to emphasise the necessity of finding "new international approaches to asylum processing and protection". The new approach of Tony Blair, the British Prime Minister, was a better regional management and the establishment of Transit Processing Centres (TPC) as he had already stated in a confidential and unfinished government plan "A new vision for refugees" of the 5th of February 2003 that was leaked to the press. Another UK plan on this matter was leaked to the press at the beginning of March 2003 (Noll 2003: 3–4). The existence of those unpublished documents was confirmed in different papers, but untraceable for me. Anyway, Tony Blair officially talks about his plans in a revised version in a letter to the Greek Prime Minister (Blair 2003).

3.1.1 Letter to Costas Simitis – the presentation of Tony Blair's new approaches

On the 10th of March 2003, Tony Blair wrote a letter to His Excellency Mr. Costas Simitis, the Prime Minister of Greece, and sent copies of it to the other members of the European Council. In the letter, he focused on the need for achieving "better management of the asylum process globally" (Blair 2003) and had already enclosed his ideas to the letter.

The reason why Tony Blair sees the absolute necessity of new asylum policies lies in the results of four areas that are marked by failure. First of all, there is a great imbalance in the support of various types of refugees. While those staying in their home countries receive an average of $50 a year, asylum seekers in Europe run up costs of up to 10,000$ a year. Moreover, the current asylum system finances criminal organisations since there is almost no way to enter Europe legally. Therefore, to reach the goal ´Europe`, most of the refugees need to take illegal steps which also means for them that they often need to spend all the money that is available to them on it. Another criticism of the current system is that it has to process so many claims that do not meet at all the criteria of full refugees.

A lot of those arriving in Europe and consequently applying for asylum burden the national asylum system since they are for example "only" economic migrants, while on the other hand, 12 million genuine refugees exist that are mostly placed in their home countries. Finally, all those failures cause a decline in the public comprehension of asylum. The aim of the UK proposal is to find a better way of managing asylum so that unfounded applications decrease and protection of genuine refugees increases (Blair 2003). David Blunkett expresses this goal by saying: "My vision is of a refugee protection and asylum processing system that is fit for the 21st century" (UK Home secretary 2003). This objective shall be reached by improving regional management and by installing processing centres outside the EU. In the words of the UK plan: Regional Protection Areas (RPA) and Transit Processing Centres (TPC).

Regional Protection Areas

For those in temporary danger because of conflict in their home country, there should be possibilities to be protected in so called Regional Protection Areas close to their home countries so that they can be sent back home as soon as the conflict situation is over. In the proposal, this idea is based on four elements:

- The conflict should not take place. That means that the EU needs to do conflict prevention work.
- The protection in the region must be improved since most of the refugees in the world stay near their home countries. But since the protection in such areas is often not at a high level, the incentive to flee to Europe is very present. So the idea is that the protection in the area needs to be enhanced to provide for people from fleeing to Europe.
- The UK proposal aims to install legal channels of migration so that genuine refugees may come to Europe without depending on criminal organisations. This would be organised on a quota basis.
- Possibilities of refugee return shall be developed. That means that those having unfounded applications could be sent back to the RPA's until the conflict in their home country is ended.

What remains absolutely unclear is if protection in the region also includes the possibility that refugees are transferred to such protection areas for the period of their asylum procedure which is how it is planned in transit processing centres (Blair 2003).

Transit Processing Centres

Transit processing centres, as extra-territorial camps are called in the UK proposal, could be installed on transit routes to Europe. Those coming to Europe illegally and seeking asylum could be moved to such centres outside the EU where their asylum claims are processed. If refugee status is granted, they can finally come to Europe legally where they are distributed to different countries on a burden sharing basis. If not, they would be sent back to their home countries unless it is not safe. In this case, a limited stay in Europe might be permitted. The procedure is uncertain if illegal immigrants are caught on their way to Europe. The question whether they should also have the possibility to seek asylum in such centres is not answered in the proposal.
The organisation of Transit processing centres could be taken over by the International Organisation of Migration (IOM) and financed by Member States. The UK proposal also plans to work with the European Commission (Blair 2003).

3.1.2 The EU response

The Brussels European Council

On the 20th and 21st of March 2003, eleven days after disseminating his proposals, Blair attended the European Council in Brussels. There, as demanded in the abovementioned letter, the presidents and prime ministers of the European Union invited the European Commission to write a report on Tony Blair's suggestions in cooperation with the UNHCR (United Nations High Commissioner for Refugees) in June 2003 (European Council March 2003: Art. G.63).

Report of the European Commission

On the 3rd of June 2003, the European Commission releases a report on the UK proposal, "Towards more accessible, equitable and managed asylum systems", as invited during the Brussels European Council. In part II "Analysis of the UK proposal" no opinion on it is forwarded, because there are still a variety of questions that "need to be researched and answered before taking any further position". Those questions deal with the procedures, the complementarity versus the substitution of the current systems and the compatibility with international and national law. Besides, it needs to be clarified whether such TPC should be inside or outside the EU. In the conclusion the emphasis is put on the fact that new approaches shall not substitute but complement the current European Asylum System. The Commission itself focuses on Protected Entry Procedures (PEP) and Resettlement schemes (Commission of the European Communities 2003). Protected Entry Procedures make it possible to seek asylum at embassies or diplomatic agencies in third countries. If granted, the asylum seeker receives an entry permit. Currently, five EU Member States already use these procedures: Austria, France, the Netherlands, Spain and the UK. Denmark revoked the system in 2002 (Fagerlund et al. 2002: 3-4).

As a short evaluation: The Danish Human Rights Centre feasibility study, published in 2002, came to the conclusion that PEP's should be introduced on a European level not as a substitute, but as a complement to the existing system (Fagerlund et al. 2002: 5). Amnesty International agrees that the idea may be good in some cases, but does not address the asylum problem globally. Furthermore, Justice[13] emphasises the complementarity, that is, PEP's must be complementary and must not have any impact on the individual processing of spontaneous arrivals. The UK government and the EU Committee of the House of Lords estimate that PEP's are not very productive (House of Lords 2004: 32, § 89). Nevertheless, the EU Commission follows the recommendation of the feasibility study of the Danish Human Rights Centre that was launched in 2000 by the EU Commission. In other words, the Communication demands PEP's as a complement to the current system of spontaneous arrivals.

Current state

In a draft of a Commission Communication (COM (2005) yyy final[14]) released in May 2005 the possibility of a European external solution seems to be reaffirmed. The paper does not only demand a "study on joint processing of asylum applications within the Union" but also outside the EU. In the Commission's words: " A Study to be conducted in close consultation with the United Nations High Commissioner for Refugees (UNHCR), on joint processing of asylum applications outside the EU territory". Both studies should be finished within 2006 (COM 2005: 15, 2.3

[13] Justice is an independent legal human rights organisation founded in 1957. For further information view www.justice.org.uk

[14] Since this source is a draft diffused by the newsletter of the Justice and Home Affairs Council, the number of the Commission Communication was not given.

Common European Asylum System). I assume that the study on processing outside the EU does not only contain the concept of external reception camps, but also that of Protected Entry Procedures.

The most recent Commission Communication "on regional protection programmes" was released on the 1st of September 2005 and represents the reaction demanded in November 2004 by the European Council. The latter asked the Commission to elaborate an action plan on pilot regional protection programmes (Commission of the European Community 2005: 10). Therefore, the Commission Communication focused on the crucial activities of regional protection schemes and on the potential host countries. Especially important seems to be the introduction of an efficient procedure to determinate the refugee status in order to help the host countries to emphasis on genuine refugees. This may be interpreted as the aim of asylum procedures outside the European Union. Moreover, EU Member States may offer resettlement to refugees on a voluntary basis to express the partnership elements of the regional protection schemes (Commission of the European Community 2005: 11). Furthermore, the European Commission proposes potential host countries as the Ukraine, Moldova, Belarus, Afghanistan, sub Saharan Africa, the Horn of Africa and North Africa (Commission of the European Community 2005: 12-14).

3.1.3 The UNHCR response

As a reaction on the UK proposal, the UNHCR presents a three-pronged model on the 17th March 2003. Its regional prong is very similar to UK's Regional Protection Areas. Secondly, its domestic prong, a summary of already communicated ideas to improve national asylum systems by accelerating and simplifying the asylum procedures. The third prong, the EU one, focuses on the installation of reception camps with the difference that they would be placed within the EU. For further details view point 3.2.

3.1.4 The EU Member State responses

The UK proposal was especially supported by the Dutch and the Danish governments. These three nations had an Intergovernmental Conference (IGC) in Denmark on the 23rd of April 2003 to further discuss extra-territorial processing. Strong opposition came from Sweden and Germany. While Sweden continued to criticise the idea with the Justice and Home Affairs Council on the 5th and 6th of June 2003, Otto Schily, the German Home minister, changed his mind and supported the proposal. The

Swedish Minister of Migration once again expressed at this Council that it was difficult to understand why the UNHCR backed up the idea (Viusa 2004).

3.1.5 The Danish Memorandum

On the 23rd of April 2003, an informal IGC[15] meeting of Denmark, the UK, the Netherlands, the EU Commission, IOM and UNHCR on the "New approaches to asylum processing and protection" was held in Denmark. The results were summarised in the so-called "Danish Memorandum"[16], a paper that was written by the Danish Ministry of Refugee, Immigration and Integration Affairs (Noll 2003: 15). The paper described the prerequisites of introduction of both Protection Zones and Transit Processing Centres as readmission agreements between host country, destination country and country of origin. Furthermore, it is emphasised that the responsibility for the maintenance would be shared between the destination country, the host country, UNHCR and IOM, while the distribution of legal accountability is not specified. Concerning the financial aspect, it is assumed that the costs will be compensated for by the savings due to the decrease in the number of spontaneous arrivals in the host country (Noll 2003: 18–19).

Protection Zone

The name of "Regional Protection Area" was changed into "Protection Zone" (PZ) and defined as a "zone in a country in the region close to a specific country of origin offering effective protection to refugees and displaced persons" (Danish Memorandum 2003: 1 in Noll 2003: 15). This effective protection means at least "a non-refoulement guarantee, physical protection and an appropriate level of social protection" (Danish Memorandum 2003: 2 in Noll 2003: 16). As in the UK proposal, it remains unclear whether asylum procedures for EU countries as planned for the TPCs will be possible in PZs. However, the problems of determination procedures were discussed; a clear answer was not given. The necessity

[15] The IGC does consultations and information exchange in the area of refugees, migration and asylum. Participants are governments (Australia, Austria, Belgium, Canada, Denmark, Finland, Germany, Ireland, Italy, the Netherlands, Norway, Spain, Sweden, Switzerland, the United Kingdom, the United States), inter-governmental organisations, the UNHCR and the IOM.

[16] This Memorandum dates from the 24th of April 2005. Since it was not available for me, as all the other IGC documents, this chapter is based on the secondary information in Noll 2003.

of a refugee status determination procedure depends on the negotiations with the host countries. Besides, it is explicitly written that "in several situations" such procedures are not necessary. It is possible, estimates Noll, that group inclusions are done. If this would also include some form of group rejection, the first question that arises is on which criteria such group rejections would be based. This cannot be easily answered. Nevertheless, some sort of individual procedures seem to be foreseen, because it is written that decisions must be taken "on the basis of selection criteria developed in close cooperation with UNHCR and with due consideration to the characteristics of the individual refugee situation" (Danish Memorandum 2003: 3 in Noll 2003: 16–17).

Transit Processing Centre

Contrary to the RPA, the designation of the TPC is taken over. The location of TPCs is not specified even if it seems that the aim is to create a setting outside the EU. Here, there is no rapprochement to the UNHCR proposal, because the Danish Memorandum supposes that "if standards are acceptable, UNHCR would be less worried with regard to whether a TPC is placed inside or outside the Union". On the contrary, the criteria for transfer to a TPC are specified by nationality, undocumented arrival and the possible place of application. Especially the first criterion is based on the UNHCR proposal. The asylum seekers belonging to those nationalities producing a high number of unfounded claims shall be sent to a TPC. In this connection, the Danish Memorandum talks about nationalities with a rejection rate of more than 90 per cent.

Regarding the legal safeguards, it is written that asylum procedures do not have to be similar to those currently used in the national states. Here, it refers to the Australian South Pacific Solution (described in 3.4.1), that uses "a quicker system based on administrative review instead of Australian jurisdiction". Other details given on the possible system are similar to the UNHCR proposal such as the idea of first instance decisions that are taken in the TPCs by staff of the destination countries. The monitoring then should be done by an independent body including UNHCR and possibly government members. To conclude, the Danish Memorandum repeats the deterrent character of facilities (Danish Memorandum 2003: 5 in Noll 2003: 17–18).

3.2 UNHCR's three pronged proposal – a response to Tony Blair's camp plans

As a reaction on the UK proposal, the UNHCR stated a three-pronged model on the 17th of March. The only information that existed at that moment was a one-page table depicting the model. The UNHCR idea wants to install three different branches, each of them covering different categories of persons seeking asylum. The regional prong aims to improve protection in the region of origin, the domestic prong continues with the national asylum systems and the EU-prong describes EU reception centres where a certain category of applicants are sent to immediately. Detailed comments on the regional and the EU prong were published in April 2003, on the domestic prong in June 2003.

3.2.1 The regional prong

The goal of this prong is a better protection in the region of origin that could be reached by considering some main issues. First of all, a better-managed global system (i) needs an amendment of neither the 1951 Geneva Refugee Convention nor its 1967 Protocol. What is needed is cooperation between the involved nation states, non-governmental organizations and international organisations to finally reach a burden-sharing system. But, at the same time, the UNHCR emphasizes the importance of the maintenance of the State responsibility. Besides, asylum seekers should not be detained except if it is necessary to "verify identity" or "to protect national security and public order". Finally, the UNHCR states that responsibility may be transferred from one state to the other provided that admission, non-refoulement, the right to seek and enjoy asylum and treatment compatible with international standards are guaranteed (UNHCR April 2003a: 1; B).

How to reach better solutions for the regions of origin? Here, the UNHCR proposes support especially for developing countries. This would have two consequences. They could provide better protection for those in need, which would result in a reduction of secondary movements. Moreover, fewer people would accept the offers of traffickers and smugglers. Another element of the regional prong consists of "the 4 R's (Repatriation, Reintegration, Rehabilitation and Reconstruction) which aim to bring together humanitarian and development actors in order to facilitate sustainable reintegration and bridge the transition period between emergency relief and long-term development". Furthermore, the UNHCR talks about "admissibility procedures" that decide whether the destination country or the country of first asylum is responsible by basing it on various factors. For example, previous stay would probably lead to the responsibility of the country of first asylum. However, family members in the destination country or the fact that the country of first asylum can not handle the influx of asylum seekers would signify a responsibility shift to the destination country (UNHCR April 2003a: 2-3; C.).

3.2.2 The EU prong

The EU prong would fight against the abuse of asylum systems. Especially economic migrants apply for asylum within a European country having unfounded claims, which costs a lot of money and denies those who really need help the potential places.
Another difficulty of the current system concerns the non-refugees that are not willing to return. The UNHCR is convinced that these problems may be solved without breaching the international law. To solve the problem, asylum seekers coming from countries that mainly produce economic migrants are immediately transferred to EU reception centres being placed close to the EU borders. Not transferred are sick people and unaccompanied minors. The centres shall be closed reception centres even if the UNHCR is against detention, but "closed reception centres will be difficult to avoid unless there is no fear of absconding and irregular movement in a particular case". Here are some further details concerning the responsibility:

- National asylum officers and second instance decision makers shall finish the processing within one month. The monitoring is taken over by the UNHCR – details are not defined yet.
- The States and international organizations shall manage the centre.
- The centre shall be financed by joint EU funding.
- The return of the people is the duty of the EU and its Member States. Here, it is very important to conclude agreements beforehand.
- Finally, those granted refugee status are redistributed among the Member States. The residence of family members and cultural reasons are taken into consideration.

The aim of limiting the abuse by economic migrants will be reached by deterrence – one month procedures in closed camps almost outside of the EU do not represent a grand incentive for economic migrants to come to Europe. Another positive impact of such a EU-wide approach is the burden sharing mechanism. Up to now, asylum remains a very national matter. Therefore burden-shifting is still the reality. Added to that, the EU would get closer to a Common European Asylum System. The UNHCR admits some disadvantages. First of all, the EU prong does neither address the problem of illegal immigration nor of those people who cannot be identified. Secondly, the UNHCR fears that debating such proposals could influence negatively those countries that, at present, do not face difficulties in asylum matters (UNHCR April 2003b: 2-3, C. and E.).

3.2.3 The revised EU-prong proposal

On the 22nd of December 2003, a revised and more detailed EU-prong was published by the UNHCR since the first proposal was not very well received. The emphasis was put on a clearer administrative structure and on the shifting of processing from the national to the European level.

A clearer administrative structure

The long-term goal is EU processing under EU authority, but to begin with, an "inter-State processing" under national law would be the reality. To reach the long-term objective, a European Asylum Agency with offices in different Member States would be required. Initially, staff would be recruited from national agencies, but gradually, an independent recruiting system will replace it. The functions of such an Agency would first be limited to support, expert advice, training and the provision of information for national staff. Slowly, it would also take over the pre-screening and registration of asylum seekers to finally decide in the first instance and to coordinate the distribution of refugees between the Member States and the return of those not in need. Added to that, an independent EU Asylum Review Board will be installed and managed.
The structure of the EU Reception Centres remains almost as aforementioned. The great difference is that the centres would be open and not closed centres, with the exception of manifestly unfounded cases. Furthermore, it is explained why the Reception Centres would be installed at the borders of the EU and not in a country placed in the centre of the EU. The stated reason is that reception and return of asylum seekers is assumed to be easier at the borders of the EU (UNHCR December 2003: 64–66).

Procedures

The details in this part concern the pre-screening/registration and the decision-making process. At the beginning, this will be handled by national officers with help form the EU Asylum Agency, but will steadily be shifted to the EU Asylum Agency and in case of appeal to the EU Asylum Review Board. Furthermore, the group of asylum seekers that is immediately sent to EU Reception Centres consist of more than only those coming from economic migrant producing countries.

What is new is that if there are too many spontaneous arrivals to a certain Member State, it will be unburdened by sending claimants to the Reception Centre. A similar widening also happened relating to the distribution of those granted asylum. There are not only family, educational and cultural ties that are taken into consideration, but also the "absorption capacity" of a Member State. Furthermore, the fact of being the host country of a Reception Centre shall be granted. All in all, the European Refugee Fund shall assist in integrating refugees.

Finally, the role of the parties involved is specified. The NGO's would give advice. IOM would additionally assist in returning rejected asylum seekers as mentioned above. The UNHCR's role comprises monitoring, giving advice, sharing data and training. In the future, it will support the EU asylum Agency and the EU Asylum Review Board (UNHCR December 2003: 61-64). To better understand the EU-prong view figure 1.

The next steps

To reach the aforementioned EU prong, it is important that EU Reception Centres, a EU Asylum Agency and a EU Asylum Review Board are established and that criteria for the distribution of those in need of protection and for the joint return of rejected cases are defined. As well as that, the legal framework must be adapted so that national and EU law on asylum questions will be compatible (UNHCR December 2003: 64-65).

3.2.4 The domestic prong

It is noted that the ideas put forward here are not new, but the domestic prong needs to be mentioned to present the complete approach. This prong aims to improve the quality of national asylum systems by accelerating and simplifying the current procedures. This shall be reached by using a single procedure and by endowing the system with qualified staff. Additionally, it is especially important that the information is impartial and updated centrally, so that the repetition of work on information on a national level is avoided. A further proposal from the UNHCR is to produce guidelines drawn out of old cases so that similar applications are processed faster.

Figure 1: The EU prong (UNHCR December 2003: 67)

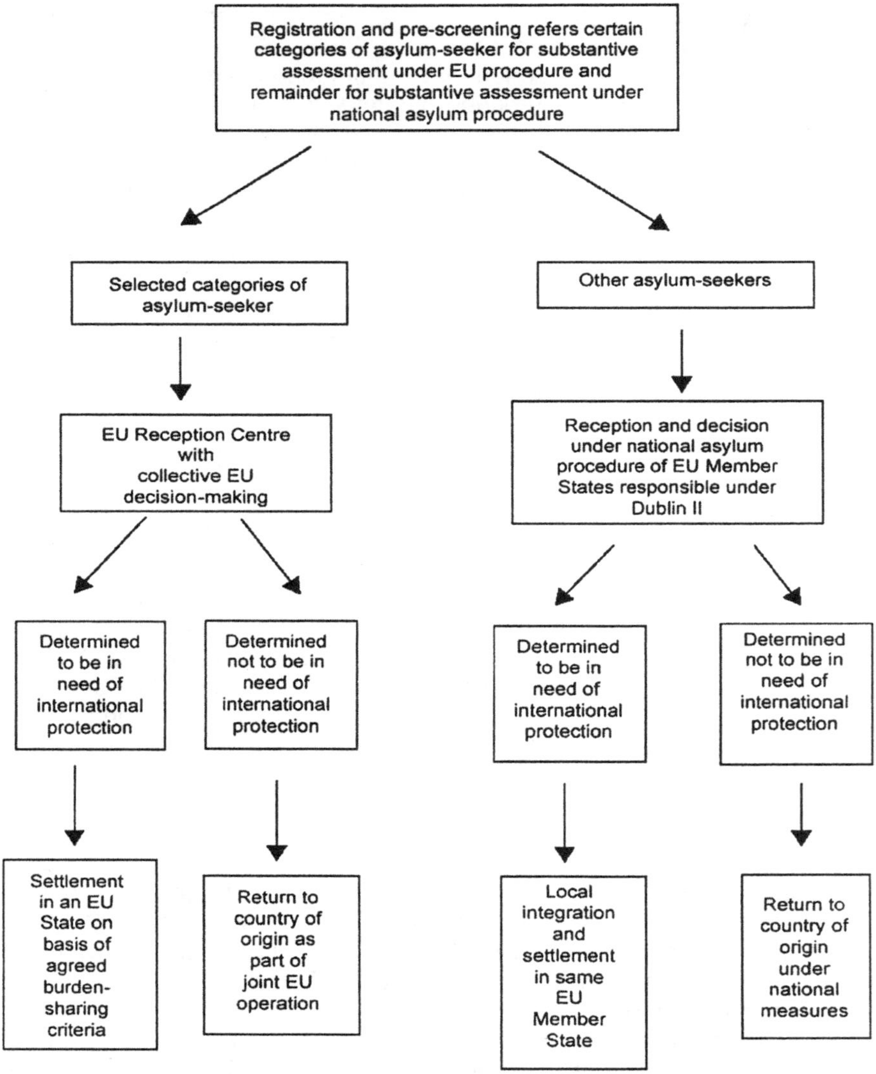

UNHCR Geneva
22 December 2003

Accelerating means in this connection that a procedure shall be finished within three months unless there are complications. Finally, the UNHCR emphasises that a broader political and social approach is essential. That means that different groups, especially media and politicians, should try to communicate the right picture of asylum seekers including the positive impacts they may have on domestic society and the economy (UNHCR June 2003: 9-10).

3.3 Otto Schily's contribution to the asylum debate – reception camps in Northern Africa

"Africa's problems must be solved within Africa," ("Afrikas Probleme müssen in Afrika gelöst werden") says German Home Minister in his article in the FAZ (Frankfurter Allgemeine Zeitung). This statement represents an argument for his proposition to externalise asylum procedures (Schily 2004). It was at the Council of Justice and Home Affairs, on the 19th of July 2004, when the Dutch presidency requested ideas concerning a common asylum policy. Otto Schily proposes the installation of reception camps in northern Africa. According to his spokesman, this is just an idea and no actual concern of government (FAZ.NET 21 July 2004). Prior to the presentation of the specifics of his proposal, it is necessary to present the background.

3.3.1 Background of Schily's proposal – the drama of the Cap Anamur refugees

The impulse for the idea of reception camps in Northern Africa gives the German relief organization Cap Anamur (headquarters in Cologne, founded by Rupert Neudeck in 1979). On the 20th of June, 2004, their lifeboat rescued 37 African refugees whose ship was in distress in the Mediterranean Sea. Ten days later, on the first of July, it attempted to enter the Sicilian port of "Porto Empodocle". But their entry was prevented by the Italian Navy, and the ship was turned back to sea. The situation on the rescue boat deteriorated and the media reported that African refugees were trying to jump ship. After eleven days, the ship was finally allowed to call on the port where the captain, Stefan Schmidt, the head of Cap Anamur Elias Bierdel and the Russian first officer were arrested. The charge was assistance to illegal immigration. Moreover, an argument about the responsibilities regarding asylum applications followed. Since it was the German crew who were accepting asylum applications, Germany was told to take responsibility (Kreickenbaum 2004). The German Home

Minister criticized the behaviour of the crew, claiming they shouldn't have accepted the applications. On the other hand, Karl Kopp, the European expert of Pro Asyl, a German working pool for refugees, countered with a press release on the 15th of July stating that since the ship was in international waters, there was no reason why the refugees should not apply for asylum to a German crew which is operating under German laws (Kopp 2004). Nevertheless, the responsibility was transmitted to Italy on the grounds that the refugees first stepped on Italian territory. But Italy was convinced that Malta was responsible for those refugees since before coming to Italy, the lifeboat cruised through Maltese territorial water. Malta answered: "Send them to Libya!" (Kreickenbaum 2004). A couple of days later, on the 22nd of July, the majority of the Cap Anamur-refugees were flown out to Africa (Braun 2004).

Shipwrecked persons on the Mediterranean Sea are very common, but it was unusual that there was such exceptional coverage in the international media. That is probably one of the reasons why Otto Schily proposes reception camps in northern Africa at this moment – the presence in the media of this drama makes it clear to everybody that there is a great necessity to increase the safety for African refugees.

3.3.2 More safety for African refugees – what should reception camps à la Schily look like?

It has to be said that there is, contrary to Tony Blair's idea, no paper giving detailed information about reception camps à la Schily. Therefore this chapter is based on statements cited in newspaper articles.

In his article in the FAZ from the 23rd of July 2004 Schily puts emphasis on the absolute necessity to increase the safety of African refugees. At the same time, he criticizes the possibility that distressed refugees are automatically received in Europe after being rescued at sea. That would just give a wrong incentive – more Africans would plunge into the sea to reach Europe. Therefore, he argues, it is essential to bring back shipwrecked people to their home country or at least to a transit country. Nevertheless, Schily is conscious that the migration pressure will continue to exist as long as there are differences in opportunities and welfare between Europe and Africa. At any rate, African problems must be solved in Africa, because Europe is not able to accept all refugees. That is one of the reasons why an externalisation of asylum procedures is imperative.
The installation of reception centres would have an impact in various ways. First of all, the EU would be freed of all those refugees that have to

be sent back because of the lack of refugee status. Second, African refugees would not need to do the dangerous crossing to apply for asylum. They could do so directly in Africa and the numerous deaths on the Mediterranean Sea would be brought to an end. "The death of a lot of people could be avoided. Is that so terribly inhuman?" asks Otto Shily ("Der Tod vieler Menschen könnte so vermieden werden. Ist das so schrecklich inhuman?). The safety aspect does play an important role in his argument. Another argument for externalising refugees is the fact that it is better for them to be interred close to their home countries, especially in cases of short term war and catastrophe. However, as Schily admits, every country is free to accept refugees on a voluntary basis (Schily 2004).

On the 3rd of August 2004, some details regarding the functioning of such reception camps were given in a FAZ article. It is written that claimants should be able to apply for asylum in the EU directly in the camp. The processing of the claim should be done by EU functionaries, so that this could represent some kind of EU asylum authority. Moreover, Otto Schily states that a control of such a procedure made by the European Court of Justice is not necessary since those camps would be outside the EU (FAZ 3 August 2004).

Several critics are objecting, especially the German green party "Die Grünen" along with a variety of human rights organisations. Therefore, Schily has revised his statements by talking about a EU branch office for a trial. He defends the idea of such installations by citing a position paper of the EU Commission from June 2004. This paper emphasised that it is essential to support the transformation of so-called transit states into safe first-asylum countries. But reception camps and branch offices are not seen as alternatives to reach this goal. There are rather planned new resettlement programs for persons in need of protection in third countries. Schily, in contrast, wants to grant asylum only in exceptional cases (Gaserow 2004). A justification of his idea based on the EU position paper seems therefore very difficult.

3.3.3 Reactions on Otto Schily's idea

(The functions of the people mentioned above correspond to their positions at the time when they were cited.)

In turn, the reactions to Otto Schily's idea are presented in detail to state one example of how politicians and different organisation react on the externalisation idea. The reason why I chose to introduce the specific reactions to Otto Schily's idea is the fact that they are the most recent. Surprisingly, a division into persons rejecting and persons backing Otto Schily's idea is not easy. You could say that in principle human rights organisations and relief organisations criticise his idea but even among them, there are some that support it. Even more difficult to assign are the political parties. However, the following paragraph tries to state some pro and contra opinions.

The German pros

The German chancellor Gerhard Schröder (SPD – Sozialdemokratische Partei Deutschlands), the Bavarian Home Minister Günther Beckstein (CSU – Christlich Soziale Union) and the foreign politician Hans-Ulrich Klose (CDU – Christlich Demokratische Union) support the idea. As you can see, Otto Schily finds support through representatives of a variety of parties. Barbara John (CDU) estimates such reception camps as the "only alternative to drowning". Even Rupert Neudeck, the founder of the German relief organisation Cap Anamur, props up the idea, because the asylum problem is growing and therefore it is essential to find "unconventional solutions" (Frankfurter Allgemeine Sonntagszeitung 25 July 2004: 1). Another representative of a relief organisation, the president of the German Red Cross Rudolf Seiters, does not want an unwise rejection of Schily's proposal because migration should already be controlled in Africa (FAZ 27 July 2004). However, those supporting the idea are reserved. In contrary, the statements of those opposing the idea are a lot clearer.

The German opponents

Claudia Roth (delegate of the green party) criticises that an externalisation does not correspond to the positions of the red-green coalition so far. Sebastian Edathy (delegate of the SPD) describes the debate as "artificial" and "superfluous", Rainer Funke (FDP) as an attempt to "undermine the right to asylum" (FAZ.NET 21 July 2004). Wolfgang Schäuble (CDU) and Guido Westerwelle (FDP) reject the idea as well (Süddeutsche Zeitung 26 July 2004). Pro Asyl, a German working pool for refugees, says that the realisation of such camps is impossible because they would break with international law. Volker Beck (parliamentary secretary of the German green party) also states legal arguments. In his opinion, reception camps outside the EU would presuppose EU asylum law that does not exist (FAZ.NET 21 July 2004). In a letter from Sebastian Müller of the Gustav-

Heinemann-Initiative to Otto Schily, he is asked to withdraw his proposal since it is "wrong, legally questionable and detrimental to the political climate in Germany ". This letter was supported by "Aktion Courage", "Humanistische Union" and "Internationale Liga für Menschenrechte" (Müller 2004). Further rejection was expressed by Katja Maurar (Medico International) and Tilman Zülch (Gesellschaft für bedrohte Völker, Society for threatened peoples). The latter emphasises that this idea is „an invitation for dictatorial states to intern refugees. That is a pervert alternative to the flight over the sea" (Hass 2004).

Two months later, at the end of September 2004, coordinated party-specific positions were stated. On the 29th of September 2004, Otto Schily puts his idea into concrete form in front of the German parliament. The resulting opinions may be summarised as follows: on principle CDU, CSU and SPD back his plan, while the green party and FDP are still doubtful about it. But all parties agree that Otto Schily would need to present a detailed. The relief organisation Pro Asyl and the human rights organisation Amnesty International stay with a full rejection of the idea.

3.3.4 Current state

During the press conference on the 9th of September 2005, Otto Schily presented a new paper on EU reception camps on the occasion of the informal meeting of the European Council of Justice and Home Affairs ministers in Newcastle. The six-page long paper mostly describes facts and ideas that were already presented in this paper such as details of the UK proposal, the UNHCR three-pronged model and the different EU Commission Communications. Furthermore, it is repeated that the asylum procedures in an EU reception facility ("EU Aufnahmeeinrichtung") as Otto Schily calls it now would only be realised on a voluntary basis and would need to be separated from asylum procedures in EU Member States (Otto Schily 2005: 4).
A new detail seems concerning the resettlement emerged. The recognized refugees would be sent back to "secure countries in the region of origin" ("sichere Länder in der Herkunftsregion"), while those not granted refugee status would be sent back to "the country of origin or the region of origin" ("das Herkunftsland oder die Herkunftsregion") (Otto Schily 2005: 4). The opportunities of unrecognised refugees and those granted refugee status in an EU reception facility à la Schily seems to be very similar.

3.4 The idea is neither new nor a European speciality

Talking of "new approaches", the proposals of Tony Blair, the UNHCR and Otto Schily seem to be new solutions that absolutely need to be implemented. But we "are served old wine in new caskets. Transit Processing Centres have been invented, implemented and evaluated before" (Noll 2003). Extra-territorial processing has already been in use by the Australian government since September 2001 under the name "South Pacific solution". It was their solution to the increasing number of economic and illegal migrants. By sending all asylum seekers intercepted en route to camps on Nauru and Papua New Guinea and the south pacific region, Australia wants to deter others of attempting to arrive illegally (BBC 2002). Furthermore, in the mid 1990s, the United States did extra-territorial processing first on the hospital-ship "USNS Comfort" and then in Guantanamo where initially Haitian and later also Cuban refugees arrived (US Navy 2005). The idea of externalisation has itself already existed for 20 years. In 1986, it was suggested by the Danish government. It proposed to install United Nations processing centres in the region to where asylum seekers would be sent if they arrived illegally to other countries. A couple of years later, at the Fifth Conference of European Ministers responsible for Migration Affairs (held in Athens in 1993), the Dutch State Secretary of Justice Aad Kosto initiated a discussion about a "system where all asylum seekers would be sent back to reception centres in their own region of origin for the processing of their claims"(Noll 2003: 8). And again, in 2000, the idea was stated by Jack Straw, UK Home Secretary, at a conference in Lisbon. Processing close to, or in the regions of origin would lead to a reduction of illegal entry and as a consequence stem trafficking and smuggling. Soon after Straw's positive remarks on externalisation, on the 22nd of November 2000, the European Commission wrote in its Communication to the European Parliament and the Council that "processing the request of protection in the region of origin" will offer "rapid access to protection without refugees being at the mercy of illegal immigration or trafficking gangs". Nevertheless, the Commission was conscious that a variety of problems needed to be solved before. Therefore, it demanded a feasibility study about extra-territorial processing (Catz et al. 2003: 45). This short step back into history shows that neither the idea nor the realisation of externalisation of asylum procedures is new. Talking about "new approaches" as it did the UK proposal is therefore misleading. To benefit from the existing experiences, the Australian and the US reality will be presented below.

3.4.1 Australia's South Pacific Solution

The background, the argumentation and the resulting idea of externalisation like Otto Schily presented it in July 2004 is a reminder of John Howard's Pacific Solution three years before. On the 26th of August 2001, 400 people[17] trying to get to Australia on an Indonesian fishing boat were rescued in the Indian Ocean by a Norwegian ship called Tampa (BBC 2002). Like the Cap Anamur in July 2004 in Italy, Tampa was not allowed to land somewhere on Australian territory even if the situation on the boat was very bad. Besides, an argument over the responsibility between Australia, Indonesia and Norway followed. Unlike the Cap Anamur, Tampa never arrived in Australia, the asylum seekers finally stranded in Papua New Guinea and Nauru (Amnesty International 2002: 1). To solve the problem of the increasing number of illegal migrants arriving in Australia, the John Howard[18] government introduced its "Pacific Solution" (also called "South Pacific Solution") in September 2001 (BBC 2002).

Only one month after the Tampa drama, in September 2001, extra-territorial processing for so-called boat people and illegal immigrants was established in the smallest republic in the world, the island Nauru, and on the Lombrum Naval Base on Manus Island in Papua New Guinea (BBC 2002). Initially, the processing was exercised by the UNHCR, but very soon, it was taken over by Australian officials, because the UNHCR was not ready to support extra-territorial processing for more than the first group of arrivals (Catz et al. 2003: 44). The goal is to deter other asylum seekers from coming to Australia by sending those trying to camps on Nauru and on Papua New Guinea. The centres were installed on these islands because other nations refused for various reasons. Fiji for example had its own problems with its racial mixed population while Tuvalu made a political statement after some of their inhabitants were not allowed to come to Australia. It is obvious that Papua New Guinea and Nauru only agreed because of the financial compensation that Australia offered. Unofficial sources speak of 15 million dollars for more than 1000 detainees on Nauru (BBC 2002). Half a year later, it is said that Nauru received 30 million dollars for hosting the asylum seekers (Macdonald 2002). In February 2002, the BBC reports of 356 claimants in Papua New Guinea

---

[17] Another source talks about 450 mostly Afghan refugees (Hiscock 2002 p 21), while a third one claims that it was exactly 438 people from mainly Afghanistan and Iraq. (Amnesty International 2002, p 1)

[18] John Howard (Liberal Party) has been Prime Minister since March 1996. He and his coalition with the National Party were elected in October 1998 and November 2001. (Microsoft Encarta Enzyklopädie Professional 2004; Australien 7.4.5)

and 1159 in Nauru (BBC 2002). By the 10th of August 2002, at least 1834 asylum seekers were sent to camps in the pacific region. The other 600 of the 2436 trying to reach Australia were forced to stay on their boats and to return to their home countries (Amnesty International 2002: 1). However, the "Pacific Solution" was criticised by a variety of organisations. Just to mention a couple of those criticisms: the breach with human rights like "the use of detention of unspecified and potentially unlimited duration without judicial review; the automatic detention of children and the detention in conditions which may be considered degrading or inhuman" was strongly criticised by Amnesty International especially because it "cannot be justified as a method of deterring potential asylum seekers" (Amnesty International 2002: 2). The Australian Immigration Minister Phillip Ruddock argues that "we cannot simply focus our energy, our resources, our compassion on people who are reaching the borders of western countries through secondary and tertiary movements; we must remember the needs of those who are further away". However, Human Rights Watch reacts that "while this is true, his belief that those further away can only be helped by means of rejecting those who come without an invitation is not" (Human Rights Watch 2002).

However, Australian's immigration policy is one of the strictest in the world. Inadequate identity papers may lead to internment as it happened to thirty-three Australians in the last two years (2003 – 2004). One Australian woman never even went back after her deportation four years ago (Wälterlin 2005: 4).

3.4.2 The United States experiences

Another example for already experienced extra-territorial processing concerns the USA. Already in 1981, the USA and Haiti signed an agreement on migration cooperation. The US Coast Guard was allowed to intercept Haitian boats with asylum seekers on it heading towards the USA and send those back that had no right to seek asylum. The determination procedure that was used was described as "the most cursory inspection". The numbers confirm it. Between 1981 and 1991, 24,600 Haitians were captured at Sea, 28 of them were allowed to apply for asylum in the USA (Newland 1995: 198). In 1991, Jean-Bertrand Aristide became the first democratically elected Haitian president which led to a short break in the immigration influx towards the States. But after a putsch on the 30th of September 1991, the influx was larger than before. Therefore, US president George W. Bush converted the US naval base at Guantanamo Bay into a so-called "processing centre". Nearly two thirds of those arriving were allowed to enter the USA. Even if a large number was allowed into the USA, the capacity of the centre was quickly exceeded. In order to deal with this, another centre was opened in Haiti where the Haitians had the possibility to apply for asylum in the USA. In the following years, the migration pressure on the USA increased (Newland 1995: 199 – 200).

In June 1994, the US asylum policy entered into a phase where it used the hospital-ship "USNS Comfort" for processing asylum applications while being placed in Kingston, Jamaica. The "Operation Sea Signal" was started with the arrival of the first Haitian asylum seekers on the 16th of June 1994. The number of people located on the ship rapidly increased to up to more than 1100. Therefore, the hospital ship brought the remaining 400 to the base in Guantanamo, Cuba, on the 16th of July 1994, only one month after the arrival of the first migrants. The Comfort was completely deactivated by 19th of August 2004 (US Navy 2005). By 15th September 1994, 14,000 Haitians were placed there (Newland 1995: 202). In the same period of time, there were some major changes in the US asylum policy towards Cuba. While for the previous 28 years Cubans were allowed to enter the States with the aim of weakening the Castro power, this argumentation was from then on used to justify exactly the contrary. In other words "the US Cold War policy of encouraging refugee flows from 'enemy' states may have done more to stabilise than destabilise unfriendly regimes. (...). The implication was that the would-be migrants should work to change the system in Cuba rather than escape from it" (Newland 1995: 191). The crucial point was the Cuban intervention on a boat trying to get to the USA, resulting in a high number of deaths. Riots in Havana followed, a mass emigration was stimulated. 35,000 people were caught on their way to Florida, another unknown number of Cubans drowned on route. As a consequence, President Clinton prohibited entry to the States, but instead offered a "safe haven" at the Guantanamo base (Newland 1995: 196 –197). Between 1994 and 1996, 50,000 boat people from Haiti and Cuba were caught and brought to camps on Guantanamo. The last Haitian migrants left Guantanamo on the 1st of November 1995, the last Cuban migrants on the 31st of January in 1996. Two other migrant operations followed. "Operation Marathon" in October 1996 and "Operation Present Haven" in February 1997 aimed at Chinese migrants attempting to reach the United States illegally (US Navy 2002).

Nowadays, a common security policy exists between Mexico and the United States. Mexico helps to control the border and the States permits Mexican guest workers to enter. The common security policy consists of the program called "Repatriación Segura" (secure repatriation) which is financed by the States and the IOM (International Organisation of Migration). This program includes detention camps at the Mexican borders where immigrants are detained for a maximum of eight hours and then sent back to their regions of origin. Thus, in 2004, Mexico sent 20,000 immigrants back. A variety of sources show that the legal maximum detention time of eight hours is not respected and the situation in the camps is very bad. In Tapachula, for example, at the Southern Mexican Border, are no beds, no showers, not even the possibility to wash one's hands and only one toilet. The camp is permanently overcrowded since its capacity is 150 persons, but usually there are 450 to 700. Rapes and violence are part of everyday life. To just state one example: in December 2001, Kanubhai Shankards Patel, an Indian migrant, committed suicide in such a detention centre because of the precarious conditions. Centres like that are not only located in Mexico, where there are 41 one of them, but also in Guatemala (south of Mexico). There, they are called "albergues" (a lodging, shelter, hostel), but the name does not change the living conditions. Not only the Mexican Camps but also those in Guatemala are financed by the United States. Juan Manuel Sandoval, a Mexican sociologist, talks of "el trabajo sucio", the "dirty work", that was externalised from the United States to Mexico, and in the meantime even to Guatemala (Zeiske 2005).

Those examples show that the countries with externalisation experiences have similar traditions regarding the treatment of asylum seekers. The USA and Australia are both typical resettlement countries who resettled a large number of their asylum seekers. The Australian and US experiences will be used – among other sources – to discuss and evaluate the externalisation of asylum procedures as solution to the asylum problem (Chapter four).

3.5 Synthesis – which burden sharing instrument corresponds to the externalisation idea?

As we have heard, extra-territorial processing was promoted with diverse focal points. The most important difference concerns the location of such reception camps. While Tony Blair and Otto Schily support processing outside the EU, the UNHCR would install them inside the borders. Whatever location for a central camp is desired, there rests a key similarity: physical transfer. Spontaneous arrivals of certain categories of asylum seekers (which vary slightly among the proposals) in a EU Member State would automatically be sent to a reception camp – either from the UK to Lybia or from France to Poland, just to state examples. Therefore, a Common EU Asylum System would not only signify simple burden sharing by policy harmonisation. Incorporating the physical transfer component would go a step further. Therefore, externalisation may be interpreted as one special kind of burden-sharing within the international community that is heading towards a split of the purchaser and the provider state. The split is not based on a specific quota, but on the categories of spontaneous arrivals (if they even succeed in arriving in Europe). However, the EU countries would become the purchaser states by financing the extra-territorial system, and the asylum processing will be realised on a territory outside the EU. As a consequence, the social and political costs (defined in Chapter two) within the EU are supposed to decrease, while the financial costs are supposed to increase. Poorer states would be paid for processing, thus for taking over the social and political costs. An overall decrease in the costs is the aim.

Hence, to place the above presented proposals of externalisation in the burden sharing debate, neither the policy harmonisation instrument nor the quota mechanisms seem to be appropriate. In other words, externalisation is not a burden sharing instrument heading towards equity, but rather towards efficiency. Nevertheless, it does not go as far as the above presented Schuck model. Even if there is a trade component in the sense of paying for the processing, there is a lack of competition between states involved so that the real preferences of the states will not be revealed via the price mechanism. However, the externalisation may be seen as a first step towards a burden sharing instrument that incorporates the market mechanism including the physical transfer of refugees. More detailed explication on externalisation as a more efficient burden sharing system (which is the aim of the abovementioned proposals) is given in Chapter 4.3.

4 The adequacy of EU reception camps

Having already described the instrument of burden sharing and the proposals of extra-territorial processing for a Common EU Asylum System in earlier chapters, this chapter will be based on an analysis of these and is divided into three parts. The first part will give a quick outline of different opinions about the proposals just to get an overview of the circulating opinions and to see who estimates externalisation to be adequate and who doesn't (4.1). But to do this we need to define what "adequate" is and what is not. Something is adequate if it is compatible with international law and principles, if it is acceptable from a humanitarian point of view, if it is politically feasible and if it reaches the envisaged aims. The second part (4.2.), based on studies, research papers and newspaper articles, will show that externalisation is not adequate from a humanitarian and legal point of view, but seems to be adequate in the sense of political feasibility. Furthermore, the adequacy of externalisation will be determined by examining it on its efficiency and equity (4.3). To do so, the economic theory will be considered. But finally the outcome will depend on the definition if the aim is a more efficient or a more equitable burden sharing system. Anyhow, since these proposals lack of details, it would not make any sense to treat each proposal separately. Therefore, the analysis in turn will concern different aspects of all three proposals with the aim to finally be able to generalise which characteristics of externalisation contribute (negatively or positively) to adequacy.

4.1 Overview of circulating opinions

4.1.1 Supporting voices by the majority of the EU Member States

The suggestion of external processing of asylum claims met with almost universal approval of the EU Member States when Justice and Home Affairs (JHA) Commissioner Vittorino presented the idea[19] at the Luxembourg meeting of the JHA Council on the 5th and 6th of June 2003. The Netherlands, Denmark and Austria openly supported the idea. Even the German Home Minister Otto Schily, who first opposed the idea, finally backed it. The only state that explicitly expressed criticism was Sweden (Statewatch 2003). Austria's consent to the "outsourcing of European refugee protection" was reaffirmed in August 2004 when Home Minister

[19] That refers to the UK and the UNHCR proposal. Schily's proposal did not exist at that moment.

Ernst Strasser expressed his wish of a reception camp for Chechen refugees in the Ukraine (Kopp 2004).

Another positive estimation of the externalisation idea was made at the Justice and Home Affairs Council in Sheveningen (Netherlands) on the 1st of October 2004. The Justice and Home Affairs ministers positively reacted on the realisation of five pilot projects in Morocco, Libya, Tunisia, Algeria and Mauritania. The idea of these pilot projects is to install reception camps in those countries where illegal immigrants are received, but where – to start with – they do not have the possibility to seek asylum. In principal, none of the ministers was against it, with open support expressed by Poland, Denmark and Italy (Viusa 2004). Another source claims that the strong supporter countries were the UK, Denmark and Italy, while France and Sweden rejected the projects (Daniel 2004). Nevertheless, the JHA ministers of the EU agreed on the elaboration of plans for the so-called "pilot projects" by the EU Commission by June 2005 (Viusa 2004). Agreeing on the planning of such camps may be interpreted as a first step towards the realisation of extra-territorial processing.

Before presenting some reputed organisations refusing externalisation plans, an important observation made by Gregor Noll, a law professor at Lund University in Sweden, shall be quoted: "States are the masters of international law." In his opinion, the realisation of state proposals is much more likely than of plans of international organisations. In other words, the Member States' judgment will have more weight in the decision- making process than the estimation of different organisations. Therefore, the abovementioned estimation of externalisation to be adequate may probably be counted more than the opponent voices in turn.

4.1.2 Voices of rejection from reputed organisations

Amnesty International estimates the three proposals as unlawful and unworkable, because they contravene international refugee law and they do not put enough emphasis on the right to seek asylum in Europe[20]. Nevertheless, it acknowledges the aim of new solutions to mixed groups of refugees and economic migrants and of better protection in poorer regions (Amnesty International 2003: 2 –3). Referring to the latter point, Amnesty International urges the Member State to "maintain and indeed increase their own protection capacity" (Amnesty International 2003: 12). Another crucial point is the fear of offending the principle of international solidarity

[20] For further details on legal estimation see 4.2.1

that would, as a consequence, result in the creation of "two classes of asylum states". On the one hand, there would be the rich countries that have the possibility to choose the number and characteristics of their immigrants. On the other hand, poor countries would need to offer protection to those that are not welcomed in the first-class asylum countries. Furthermore, illegal migration as well as exploitation by traffickers and by employers will continue. In the worst case, those really in need of protection are discouraged to seek asylum. All in all, externalisation of asylum procedures is an expensive and ineffective solution that results in the abuse of human rights. Finally, it is recommended to concentrate on resettlement schemes, protected entry procedures and the protection capacity of host states (Amnesty International 2003: 2-4).

ECRE[21] (European Council on Refugees and Exiles) appreciates that governments try to find solutions for the current failures in national asylum systems, but emphasises that they must be in conformity with Tampere and the 1951 Geneva Convention. It also welcomes, like Amnesty International, that the improvement of protection capacity of poorer regions is intended. ECRE reacts in disapproval concerning the breach of the principle of international solidarity. It is highly unfair if asylum seekers are sent to poorer regions that already deal with a larger number of potential refugees than the richer European countries. Furthermore, human rights abuse is feared because of the scant protection capacity of the envisaged regions. Like other groups who reject these ideas, ECRE is worried about legal violations[22]. In a study in cooperation with the USCR (United States Committee for Refugees)[23], it is simply summarised that "principled, legal, and practical considerations make the implementation of such ideas problematic" (Catz et al. 2003: 45).

The EU Committee of the House of Lords, like ECRE and Amnesty International, stresses the legal difficulties of the proposals because a contravention of international refugee law is very likely[24]. As a new point, it especially criticises the fact that the UK and the UNHCR proposal do not

[21] ECRE represents 74 refugee assisting NGO's working in 31 European countries towards humane und fair asylum policies and practice. It seeks to contribute to the development of a comprehensive response to the global refugee situation. For further information see www.ecre.org

[22] For further details on legal estimation see 4.2.1

[23] USCR's mission statement is "to adress the needs and rights of persons in forced or voluntary migration worldwide by advancing fair and humane public policy, facilitating and providing direct professional services, and promoting the full participation of migrants in community life". For further information see http://www.refugees.org/

[24] For further details on legal estimation see 4.2.1

clear up questions of responsibility, cost and legal. As a conclusion, it strongly recommends that solutions will be found for a faster and better processing procedure within the nation states instead of planning processing centres (House of Lords 2004: 32, § 88). In a report on the Hague programme, published on the 23rd of March 2005, the EU Committee repeated the above stated estimation and reaffirmed the necessity of improving the asylum procedures within the EU before thinking about external processing (House of Lords 2005: § 24).

A variety of social groups[25] wrote comments of rejection after the Justice and Home Affairs (JHA) Council meeting on 1st of October 2004 and thus also following the backing of the externalisation plans by the JHA ministers. The wording was: "We reject the concept of camps at the European borders. We urge heads of governments and parliamentarians to oppose it firmly. We demand that following fundamental principles based on international law, the European Union improves access to protection rather than shifting the responsibility for refugee protection on other countries" (Churches Committee for Migrants in Europe 2004).

Furthermore, the Law Society like for instance Justice[26] and the Immigration Law Practitioners' Association (ILPA)[27] formulated deep criticism of the legal regime of such reception camps. A breach of the Geneva Convention, the Universal Declaration of Human Rights, the Charter of Fundamental Rights of the European Union and the European Convention on Human Rights is feared. The problems, among others, are the responsibility transfer from one state to another, the automatic detention, and the refused right to seek asylum in the envisaged country.[28]

---

[25] First Signatories: CCME (Churches Committee for Migrants in Europe), the FIDH-AE (European Association for the Defence of Human Rights), Germany : Pro-Asyl, Belgium : MRAX (Mouvement contre le Racisme l'Antisémitisme et la Xénophobie), Great Britain : JCWI (Joint Council for the Welfare of Immigrants), Spain : SOS-Racismo, APDHA (Associacion Pro Derechos Humanos de Andalucia), France : Cimade, Gisti, LDH (Human rights League and Italian), Italy : ARCI, FCEI (Federazione delle Chiese Evangeliche in Italia), some of them participating to the MIGREUROP network. This appeal is supported by following members of the European Parliament: Daniel Cohn-Bendit (Greens), Hélène Flautre (Greens), Adeline Hazan (ESP).

[26] Justice is an independent legal human rights organisation founded in 1957. For further information view www.justice.org.uk

[27] The Immigration Law Practitioners' Association was established in 1984 by a group of leading UK immigration practitioners to represent immigrants, to provide information and to provide a non-racist, non-sexist, just and equitable system of immigration, refugee and nationality law. Today it has more than 1200 members. For further information view: http://www.ilpa.org.uk/

[28] For further details on legal estimation see 4.2

All mentioned organisations estimate externalisation to be inadequate for legal reasons. Moreover, most of them fear the non-performance of the principle of international solidarity. Those and other aspects will be discussed in turn.

4.2 Analysis on the basis of quality criteria

As explained in the introduction, the following analysis of documents uses a content analytical scheme of categories. These categories were determined on the basis of the inductive method, thus after a first lecture of the documents so that their content may be evaluated more easily. In a second step, an analysis frame was established by using the structure of the evaluation scheme of Secours Catholique, a French relief organisation. But since a framework does not meet up with all the criteria necessary to analyse the outsourcing of asylum, this frame has been revised and extended by the categories determined before. Therefore, it was possible to include legal and political criteria to be able to determine the adequacy of externalised reception camps.

However, before examining the potential of an adequate realisation of the "externalisation project", the analysis frame inspects the surroundings of the project – the authors' knowledge and circumstances. The Secours Catholique evaluation scheme asks if the social, economic, political and geographic circumstances are well known by the authors of the proposals. Since all the externalisation proposals come from bodies that may fall back on expertise within their organisations (which is the case for politicians in governments as well as for the UNHCR), this question might be answered positively.

The second introductory approach to the core of the proposal concerns the authors, their capacities and competences. The UNHCR is a non-governmental international organisation whose duty is to solve the worldwide refugee problem. The protection of refugees has to be realised by 6540 people in 116 countries[29]. This leads to the supposition that the UNHCR developed its proposal in a neutral environment that principally heads towards a better protection for refugees – at least that is its duty.

The other two proposals were born in a very political environment. Starting from the assumptions of Joseph Schumpeter, the political outcome is

[29] General information about the UNHCR available at http://www.unhcr.ch/cgi-bin/texis/vtx/basics [accessed 15 September 2005].

influenced by a variety of aspects. Joseph Schumpeter supposes that democracies work like markets. Basically this means that the demand side (the voters) determines the supply side (politicians). In other words, politicians in democracies will orientate what they supply according to the voter's attitude (Schumpeter 1955: 427f.). Using this theory, it may be assumed that Otto Schily and Tony Blair also pursue political aims. Hence, their overall goal is their re-election and probably not the protection of refugees. Therefore, ideas born in a political environment need to be examined in terms of their strategic and political background as this will be done in 4.2.5. This shows that the circumstances of the Schily and the Blair proposal are different than those of the UNHCR.

4.2.1 The aim of extra-territorial processing

How is it defined?

In principal, the objective of extra-territorial processing is to solve the asylum problem by closing the EU borders for economic migrants (limiting aspect) and by enhancing their security (security aspect). To begin with, the *limiting aspect* heads towards avoiding the entry to the EU for economic migrants. As mentioned in chapter two the asylum channel is more and more used by economic migrants since they have gradually lost the possibilities to legally enter the EU. As a consequence, the number of rejected asylum seekers increased in the last couple of years. Therefore, politicians want to find ways to select economic migrants from genuine refugees before they come to Europe. Finally, only genuine refugees would have the possibility to cross the EU borders. As a consequence, the beneficiaries would be genuine refugees who would gain access more quickly to the EU as economic migrants would block the asylum channel less and less.

A further aspect refers to *security* that is becoming more and more relevant in terms of migration policies by experts and policy makers. Especially Otto Schily links asylum matters with security by emphasising the need to decrease the number of deaths on the Mediterranean Sea. Hence, the externalisation or rather the possibility to seek asylum outside the EU would contribute to enhancing the security of asylum seekers. Here, the beneficiaries would be all persons trying to come to Europe since they would have the "chance", as the different proposals put it, to apply for asylum in the EU without exposing themselves to a dangerous journey.

Does the project react in an appropriate way to reach these aims?

Would the limiting aspect be fulfilled? Would economic migrants block the asylum channel less? It could be answered that by processing asylum claims outside of the EU, fewer economic migrants would come to Europe since their asylum claims would already be rejected in the reception camp outside the EU. Hence, before they would even come to Europe, they would be sent back to their home countries. This is very problematic because of the asylum determination procedure planned to be realised in such camps. The UNHCR proposes that it should take no more than a month and the whole process should be under public scrutiny. Furthermore, it is highly doubted if such procedures would be apt to comprehensively scrutinize each asylum claim. In other words, it is very likely that among the rejected asylum seekers would be "genuine" refugees that would not get asylum in the EU. That is a key risk that should not be neglected. Even if such procedures would be optimised and be fair, it is highly questionable if there would be this large decrease in the arrival of illegal economic migrants in the EU. For several reasons that are discussed within the following paragraph it might be assumed that immigrants will continue to arrive in the EU illegally. Hence, the desired effect of limiting illegal immigrants through externalisation would be very small.

The second question here concerns the security aspect. Taking the proposal of Otto Schily: would EU reception facilities in North Africa lead to less cases of death on the Mediterranean Sea?

A variety of people would say yes. Barbara John (CDU) as an exemplary voice agrees with Schily because she currently sees "no other way to save the lives of human beings. Such reception camps are the alternative to drowning" (Frankfurter Allgmeine Sonntagszeitung 25 July 2004). A similar statement was given in the commentary of Stefan Dietrich in the same newspaper one day earlier (Dietrich 2004). The humanity of this argumentation seems to be the crucial point for the majority of the supporters of Schily's idea.

In contrast to this, there are several voices who would negate the abovementioned statement. People would not be deterred from fleeing to Europe by sending back distressed refugees to reception camps situated outside the EU because "they do not have anything to lose". They just want to reach a better world that lies on the other side of the Mediterranean Sea (Kreickenbaum 17 July 2004). If analysed in detail, the reduction of the number of those drowning at sea would be very little. Economic migrants would very quickly know that they do not have any chance to get asylum in such reception camps. So if they were there, they would be sent back to their home countries after a certain period of time. As a result, they would avoid approaching such camps and continue to take the dangerous way to Europe via the sea. Once arrived, there is at least a small hope that they could find some work in the EU (Dietrich 2004). Furthermore, if we look at Schily's new thoughts about externalised reception camps published in September 2005, the ineffectiveness of such reception camps will be confirmed. As described in Chapter three, Schily proposes to send recognised refugees back to safe countries in their regions of origin, while unrecognised refugees would be sent to their countries of origin or their regions of origin. If the result of extra-territorial processing was to end up in the region of origin, a vast majority of asylum seekers would continue to immigrate illegally. In other words, they would continue to take a variety of risks to reach their goal Europe and a part of those would continue to die on their ways. Hence, the aim of increasing security for refugees would not be reached by installing reception facilities. Provided that this statement is true, asking how then the goal of enhanced security for refugees could be reached completes this paragraph. Some argue that the number of drowned people would be reduced if the EU Member States bordering the Mediterranean Sea did not send back old boats with refugees on them (Kreickenbaum 17 July 2004). Michael Schwelien (2005: 14-15) emphasises that the refugees' security would certainly be more enhanced if legal entry to the EU was possible. Two examples from Italy also confirm the argumentation that the security of refugees may be more easily enhanced by opening the borders than by closing them.

The first migratory fluxes arriving in Italy came from Albania. Nowadays, this movement is inexistent because of a variety of bilateral contracts between Italy and Albania. As a consequence, it is a lot cheaper and less dangerous to buy a visa at the Italian Consulate in Tirana as crossing the Sea (Miraglia 2005). This shows that open borders, and thus the possibility of legal entry to the EU, would deter refugees from arriving illegally via dangerous routes.

A second possibility to enhance the security of those trying to come to the EU would be an amendment to Italian law. Up to now, Italian fishing boats and their crews have been responsible during legal procedures for those migrants they saved at Sea. In other words, saving the life of a refugee implies for the fishermen that they need to stop working for a couple of weeks. It is more than understandable that those old boats with a lot of refugees on them are often "not seen" by the fishing boats (Miraglia 2005). These examples show that fewer deaths on the Mediterranean Sea might be the result of loosening the EU asylum laws rather than by tightening them.

Is sustainability of the project given?

Nowadays, the sustainability aspect is of high importance. Therefore, potential projects also need to fulfil the sustainability criterion. It is very likely that this is not the case when talking about externalisation. The majority of refugees being interned in a reception camp would be sent back to their country of origin and it may be assumed that their country of origin is not the place where they want to stay because otherwise they would not have left it in the beginning. Therefore, the probability of those refugees trying to come to Europe again is very high. The only difference will be that they would not approach to the reception camp anymore since their experiences tell them that the reception camp means the end of their dream of Europe.

By looking at the camps at the US-Mexican border, this statement may be underpinned. Kathrin Zeiske talks in her work about migrants being detained in the US-run deportation camps in Mexico. Manuel, a Migrant from Honduras, is one example. He was detained in the "estación migratoria" in Tapachula at the Southern Mexican border while waiting to be deported. After four days, he could not bare the detainee life anymore and agreed to get on the bus leaving for Honduras. But, a couple of days later, he came back to Mexico to once again try to enter the States. He did not have anything to lose (Zeiske 2005). It might be true that not everybody reacts like Manuel in Mexico, but I suppose that such behaviour is very likely. Statistics to underpin this statement do not exist for the moment, but could be the subject of further research. However, if we start from the assumption that a majority of migrants would do the same as Manuel because they do not have anything to lose anyway, the externalisation project would not reach sustainable goals. Sending back people does not make any sense if the majority among them come back again and again. Another solution would need to be found.

Were results of former evaluations considered?

To judge projects and their seriousness, it is important to include the results of former evaluations to give a complete picture – either to define the foundations of a new proposal or to refute its validity. None of the proposals considered former evaluations.

The Intergovernmental Consultations on Asylum, Refugees and Migration Policies in Europe, North America and Australia published a "Working Paper on Reception in the Region of Origin" in September 1994 and a draft follow-up to the 1994 Working Paper in August 1995. Since it was impossible to get access to these documents, these following paragraphs are based on citations in publications by Amnesty International and Gregor Noll. The two aforementioned IGC publications express doubt on the legal, political and humanitarian feasibility of the idea of exclusive regional processing. Gregor Noll gives a literal quotation of the conclusion of the IGC draft follow up in 1995 that shall be repeated here:

"Comments to the 1994 IGC Report from a variety of sources indicate that the suggestion of protection in an 'exclusive' location faces significant moral (political and humanitarian) and legal obstacles. Politically, it is a controversial scheme that would possibly have a very negative impact on public opinion. Moreover, it contravenes a number of relevant provisions of International Law and also seems to be incompatible with Constitutions and internal systems in many participating States. On the practical side, it may encourage human trafficking, using forged identities and nationalities. Careful examination of these impediments therefore lead to the conclusion that the 'exclusive' option is not feasible and as such, does not deserve further elaboration" (IGC 1995: 7 in Noll 2003: 9).

This paragraph shows that already ten years ago, the external solution was rejected for humanitarian, political and legal reasons. Surprisingly, the externalisation proposals did not try to disprove these counter-arguments. Relying on the forthcoming analysis of externalised reception camps, the reason for not mentioning the infeasibility results could lie in the impossibility to refute its obstacles. Gregor Noll (2003: 10) also wonders about the non-consideration of the IGC evaluation. Nevertheless, a complete approach would need to take all the concerned aspects into consideration – former evaluations as well as risks and unrealistic components.

Potential risks and unrealistic components

The UNHCR proposal is the only one that mentions several risks and deficits. First, the discussions about the problems of asylum systems risk having a negative influence on those countries which, at present, do not face difficulties with asylum seekers. Furthermore, the UNHCR criticises that its proposal does neither address the problem of illegal immigration nor of those people who cannot be identified (UNHCR April 2003b: p 2-3, C. and E.). In contrast to Blair and Schily, the UNHCR proposal may be positively emphasised here because of its partially realistic estimation. Nevertheless, there are still a variety of project risks and unrealistic (in the sense of not feasible) components that are not mentioned at all.

One important risk of the realisation of externalisation is its effect on the society of the EU. The electorate is already “simply intolerant” when it comes about the abuse of the asylum by economic migrants or insufficient border controls (Gibney 2004: 245). As the Australian example shows, the intolerance of the electorate seemed to be confirmed by the realisation of the South Pacific Solution “in a way that created even greater public hostility to asylum seekers (many of whom were genuine refugees)” (Gibney 2004: 249). Such a confirmation strengthens the EU citizens’ bad opinion of an asylum seeker, but was not at all mentioned in the proposals. Regarding the existing migration pressure and the continuing arrival of migrants, whipping up hostile emotions and tensions is an essential risk for a European society.

Furthermore, it is very unrealistic to suppose that *forced transfers* to and from reception camps would be held without any complications. On the contrary, it is even very likely that, as the experience with forced return shows, human right abuses would occur frequently (Amnesty International 2003: 21). The Comprehensive Plan of Action (CPA)[30], for instance, was based on voluntary transfers of Vietnamese boat people and shows how many difficulties may occur in this context. Amnesty International reports that tens of thousands of them were exposed to very bad treatment so that they left voluntarily. “People have been shot, beaten, forced to sleep outside without shelter, and have had only partial access to fair refugee status determination procedure” (Amnesty International 1996). It is very likely that in the EU version there would also be a certain number of asylum seekers that oppose forced transfers and, as a consequence, similar circumstances as within the CPA would occur. It is obvious that this is not the aim, but if the authors were realistic, they would have needed to consider this risk.

Assuming the option of creating *open reception camps* is a further demonstration of the fact that the reality of the situation is being ignored and that potential risks are not being presented. In its revised EU-prong proposal,

---

[30] The CPA was introduced at the 1989 held Conference on Indo-Chinese Refugees as a new approach to deal with the large amount of Vietnamese asylum seekers in the ASEAN (Association of South East Asian countries). Between 1989 and 1998, 110 000 Vietnamese boat people were repatriated. Further information available at: http://www.un.org.vn/unag/unhcr1/unhcr.htm [accessed 28 April 2005].

the UNHCR foresees open reception centres unless the claim of a refugee is manifestly unfounded. Amnesty International and the EU Committee of the House of Lords estimate that extra-territorial processing would very probably amount to detention (House of Lords 2004: 31, § 85). Besides, in its first description of the EU-prong in April 2003, the UNHCR speaks about closed reception camps. The new definition was used after closed camps had strongly been criticised. To assume open reception centres is extremely unrealistic and deliberately misleads the public. As a consequence, closed reception camps are a lot more realistic and lead to the next potential risk.

Detention of asylum seeker does not only break international law as it is described in Chapter 4.2.2, but would lead to an unfavourable environment. The low level of expected chances and the picture of the western world could easily encourage the asylum seekers staying in such camps to join certain groups. In this connection, Raekha Prasad talks in a Guardian article about such places as "a fertile ground for rebels" (Prasad 2003). Statewatch asks how people would react if they were detained in camps outside the EU and is convinced that European governments do not care about that question since "out of sight is out of mind" (Statewatch March 2003). The Australian example confirms the risk of detaining asylum seekers in such camps. It was reported in September 2002 that in the year before, there was one suicide and a riot in the Nauru camps. Besides, a lot of asylum seekers were "going out of their minds" because they did not know anything about their future. The fact that journalists and lawyers were not allowed into these facilities confirms the assumption of very bad circumstances (Macdonalds 2002). Furthermore, there is a large amount of evidence that being detained for an uncertain period of time may have a large psychological impact, especially on children (Amnesty International 2002:21). Since it is obvious that the camps in Nauru and Papua New Guinea represent a "form of detention" (Amnesty International 2002: 18), effects on the psyche as aforementioned are very probable. All in all, Australia spends a lot of resources on "punishing asylum seekers rather than the smugglers themselves" (Amnesty International 2002: 22). It may be concluded that the situation in the EU reception camp might be as bad as in Australian reception camps. The authors of the proposals do not mention this risk.

Another reproach concerns the envisaged "speed" by UNHCR. Certain categories of asylum seekers shall be *immediately* transferred to EU reception camps. After a *rapid* processing of their applications, they shall *rapidly* be returned to either the host country or the country of origin, depending on the results of the processing (Amnesty International 2003:

13). It is unrealistic to assume that transfer, processing and return will always work out rapidly without incidents. Furthermore, the rapid processing is limited to the duration of one month. Amnesty International highly questions if a reasonable procedure may be realised within one month (Amnesty International 2003: 31).

A further unrealistic part of the plan is the *definition of the group* that is automatically sent to Reception Centres. The Danish Memorandum specifies that this group shall contain those belonging to nationalities with a rejection rate of over 90 per cent. Here, it is neither said how the rejection rate is defined (different states measure differently) nor if it means the rate of one nation or the aggregate global rate. Noll estimates that the latter does make more sense. While examining the statistics of the year 2001, the following was discovered. Nationalities with global rejection rates higher than 90 per cent are Algeria, the Former Yugoslav Republic of Macedonia, Mali, Mexico, Sierra Leone, Ukraine, and Vietnam. In Europe's case this would mean that asylum seekers coming from these places would be immediately sent to Reception centres. This part of the plan has two unrealistic components. Those countries concerned do not produce a big part of the refugees coming to Europe; hence the instrument of externalisation would not contribute to a significant decrease in the number of spontaneous arrivals. Besides, asylum seekers will very quickly get this information and will not necessarily admit that they belong to such nationalities. The two other criteria for automatic transfer to a TPC are "undocumented arrival and possible place of application". Especially the criterion of undocumented arrival will affect a large number of asylum seekers, although, to be correct, it must be emphasised that "the absence of proper documentation is unrelated to protection need" (Noll 2002: 22–23).

Finally, common asylum laws across the EU are the basis for a new EU burden sharing system and an EU reception camp system that follows an EU standard. The House of Lords strongly disbelieve in a fast realisation of EU-wide common rules since the Member States already needed four years to agree on minimum standards in the asylum policy (House of Lords 2004: 30, § 81).

On the one hand, the proposals ignore a variety of risks such as detention and forced transfer. On the other hand, they are based on several unrealistic assumptions such as the workability of open camps and quick procedures. A lack in the presentation of potential risks and too many unrealistic aspects negatively influence the image of the proposals – it does not give the impression of a realistic estimation of the problem.

Up to this point, the proposals do not seem to be adequate because they do not react in an appropriate way to the aims and do not give sustainable solutions. Furthermore, they ignore former evaluations, potential risks and unrealistic components. This statement will be emphasised by the following section, the legal evaluation of extra-territorial processing, which will show that the proposals contain a diversity of unlawful aspects.

4.2.2 Are the externalisation plans lawful?

Processing outside the application country

From a legal point of view, extra-territorial processing is seen as a breach of international law. ECRE (European Council on Refugees and Exile) fears in a press release of the 17th of March 2003 that extra-territorial processing outside the EU is likely to contravene Article 14.1 of the Universal Declaration of Human Rights (ECRE 2003). The Universal Declaration of Human Rights was adopted on the 10th of December in 1948 by the General Assembly of the United Nations. Article 14.1 demands that "everyone has the right to seek and to enjoy in other countries asylum from persecution" (United Nations General Assembly 1948: Art. 14.1). Moreover, according to ECRE, extra-territorial processing could be contrary to Article 18 of the Charter of Fundamental Rights of the European Union (ECRE 2003). This article says that "the right to asylum shall be guaranteed with due respect for the rules of the Geneva Convention of 28 July 1951 and the Protocol of 31 January 1967 relating to the status of refugees and in accordance with the Treaty establishing the European Community" (European Union 2000: Art. 18).

However, The United Kingdom government argues that the idea of externalisation is not in breach of international law, because it is not specified that applications must be processed within the country of application. Not even article 1.A.(2) of the 1951 Geneva Convention does so. It demands that every state needs to protect those "owing to well-founded fear of being persecuted for reasons of race, religion, nationality, membership of a particular social group or political opinion, is outside the country of his nationality and is unable or, owing such fear, is unwilling to avail himself of the protection of that country; or who, not having a nationality and being outside the country of his former habitual residence as a result of such events, is unable or, owing such fear, is unwilling to return to it" (UNHCR 1996: 16, Art 1.A.(2)). But it does not specify that protection must be given within the country.

In a Justice-paper, Nadine Finch and Ian MacDonald affirm that this article does not lay down the "where" to process asylum applications, but regarding article 33 of the Geneva Convention, the situation changes (Finch / MacDonald 2003: §9). There, the non-refoulement-principle is defined as follows: "No Contracting State shall expel or return ("refouler") a refugee in any manner whatsoever to the frontiers of territories where his life or freedom would be threatened on account of his race, religion, nationality, membership of a particular social group or political opinion" (UNHCR 1996:32, Art. 33.1). That means that it is a question of safety whether claimants may be sent to third countries. As a consequence, TPC's may only be installed in countries where the safety is guaranteed (Finch / MacDonald 2003: §9). Therefore, the potential host countries for reception centres are limited. The EU Committee of the House of Lords shares the opinion that the 1951 Convention is not imperatively forbidding the transfer of state responsibility unless it concerns an unsafe country (House of Lords 2004: 30, § 82).

Back to Art. 14.1 of the Universal Declaration of Human Rights that demands that "everyone has the right to seek and to enjoy in other countries asylum from persecution". The law experts from Justice estimate that this also implies that the application of the asylum seeker would be at least considered in the state. Consequently, temporary admission must be offered. Therefore, an automatic removal to a centre outside the EU before considering the application would be in breach of international law (Finch / MacDonald 2003, §10 – 13). Amnesty International states a very similar line of argumentation and even enlarges it. According to this organisation, it is said in the Foreword of the UNHCR Handbook on Procedures and Criteria for Determining Refugee Status from 1979 that "the text of the Refugee Convention itself points to the conclusion that obligations are not only intended to be engaged but also delivered in the territory of a state". Besides, the state practice since the passing of the Refugee Convention in 1951 also affirms that processing shall be made in the application state (Amnesty International 2003: 20).

Obviously, the lawfulness of processing outside the application state depends on the interpretation of international law. However, it may be said that even if extra-territorial processing was legally recognised, it may only be realised within safe countries. The definition of a safe country cannot be discussed here. Nevertheless, we can conclude that in principal the processing outside the application country is – under certain circumstances – legally possible.

Transfer of responsibility

Amnesty International is convinced that the transferring state retains responsibility for the transferred person. In addition, the receiving state would also be responsible since the person on its territory would also be part of its jurisdiction. The UNHCR proposal states that no reception camp would divest a state of its responsibility and is, as a consequence, trouble-free here. Gregor Noll, an assistant professor at the University of Lund in Sweden, agrees on that point as long as the non-refoulement principle and human rights norms are valid. To enforce this opinion, he cites in his work a decision of the ECtHR (European Court of Human Rights) of 7 March 2000[31]. It states that the UK would be responsible even if asylum seekers were transferred to Contracting States of the Geneva Convention, so that the respect of Article 3 of the Geneva Convention[32], hence the non-discrimination principle, is guaranteed (Noll 2003: 19-20). The UK proposal, in contrast, foresees to limit the obligation of the transferring state by, in the worst case, withdrawing its signature from the Geneva Convention and changing Article 3 of the European Convention on Human Rights (ECHR). The latter demands no inhuman and degrading treatment and also refers to territory outside the state. Therefore, the UK would be accountable for human rights abuse on persons who originally sought asylum in the UK even if they were transferred to another territory for processing. As a result, the UK proposal says that amendments to Article 3 of the ECHR would be required in addition to the withdrawal of the refugee convention. But this is not enough, believes Amnesty International. It reproaches the authors of the UK proposal for not having considered other legal frameworks like the UN Convention on the Rights of the Child (CRC), the UN Convention against Torture and Other Cruel, Inhuman or Degrading Treatment or Punishment (UNCAT) and the International Covenant on Civil and Political Rights (ICCPR). Since they prohibit among other things discrimination and the return of someone to agony or random arrest, the transfer of responsibility for asylum seekers to other states is unlawful (Amnesty International 2003: 23–25).

Even if Amnesty International was not right, another legal difficulty of the UK proposal is seen in the envisaged responsibility shift to the UNHCR

---

[31] ECtHR (Third Chamber) "Decision as to the Admissibility of Application No. 43844/98 by T.I. (Transparency International) against the UK, 7 March 2000, unpublished, p 16. [Transparency International is a non-governmental organisation to fight against corruption. For further details see: http://www.transparency.org]

[32] "The Contracting States shall apply the provisions of this Convention to refugees without discrimination as to race, religion or country of origin." (UNHCR 1996, Art. 3, p 19)

and the IOM. The UNHCR does not have the required finances and structures to be responsible for all refugees arriving to the EU, while the IOM disposes of the needed funds and structures. That is a sign that the IOM would be able to manage asylum flows towards the EU, but it is not accountable to the UN General Assembly for its actions. In addition, it is neither bound by human rights treaties nor by legal obligations of its Member States. It is not even bound to the non-refoulement principle. Moreover, most of the countries where TPCs could be installed have not signed international treaties on human rights. A responsibility shift, even if it was lawful, would pose a variety of problems (Finch / MacDonald 2003: §19-21).

Furthermore, another problem might occur on this matter. The maintenance of state responsibility in case of externalisation does not imply the release of accountability for the host state of the reception centre. It is possible that the latter also is responsible for certain subjects, although the exact share may not be defined as long as there is no concrete example. However, this double-responsibility might impede the possibility of filing an action. As legal assistance will very likely be weak, refugees are even more limited in their legal possibilities in a "multi-actor setting, because they can not even be sure against which state the claim shall be entered" (Noll 2003: 20).

To summarise, the transfer of responsibility is unlawful. Even if this aspect of extra-territorial processing was not realised, a double-responsibility would cause a lot of problems on the side of the asylum seeker. The feasibility of extra-territorial processing decreases because of the responsibility question.

Detention

According to Human Rights Watch[33] and Justice, the automatic imprisonment in reception camps is incompatible with international law, especially with Art. 31 of the Geneva Convention (Finch / MacDonald 2003: §31). This article says that "the Contracting States shall not impose penalties, on account of their illegal entry or presence, on refugees who, coming directly from a territory where their life or freedom was threatened in the sense of article 1, enter or are present in their territory without authoriza-

[33] Human Rights Watch is an independent, nongovernmental organization that is dedicated to protecting the human rights of people around the world. For further information: http://www.hrw.org/

tion, provided they present themselves without delay to the authorities and show good cause for their illegal entry or presence" (UNHCR 1996: 31, Art. 31.1). If a person is automatically detained in a centre, as a result of his or her seeking asylum, this can be seen as a penalty and consequently as a breach of the Geneva Convention (Finch / MacDonald 2003: §31). We can conclude from this that Amnesty International openly disagrees with detention of asylum seekers unless he or she committed a criminal act or if detention may be justified in conformity with international rights for each individual case. But, unfortunately, detention is "an unavoidable element of the proposals" even if it is not foreseen as such. As a consequence, realising the externalisation plans would also imply detention. In the UNHCR case it would be limited to one month since the maximum length of processing is one month. It must be noted here that determination procedures of one month are doubted to be fair and acceptable. However, the UK proposal does not explicitly comment on the time question. Nevertheless, concerning the RPA the UK proposal does talk about further stay after the processing could lead to an unspecified period of detention as it is experienced in the "Pacific Solution" (Amnesty International 2003: 29–31).

Gregor Noll sees the possibility of "indefinite detention" also in TPC's. A prolonged detention might occur when for example the application is rejected and at the same time the readmission refused by the region of origin. Then there is no other possibility than a continuation of detention. In this case, Article 5(2) ECHR and Article 5 (4) ECHR become important. This first one requires that the reasons for detention must immediately be told in a way that the detainee is able to understand them. The latter offers the possibility of a court review on the lawfulness of detention. But Gregor Noll estimates that "a rejectee without repatriation perspective must be allowed to leave the TPC, if conflicts with Article 5 (1)(f) ECHR are to be avoided. This might lead to irregular secondary movements, which is precisely what the reform proposals aim at avoiding" (Noll 2003: 26–27). Finally it must be noted that detention does not only have legal, but also a lot of human consequences. These will be discussed further down.

The aspect of detention is illegal. Even if UNHCR proposes this in its revised EU-prong open camps, it is very doubtful if such open camps are realistic. It seems very probable that a lot of asylum seekers would try to get to Europe and will not remain in open camps. Therefore, it is assumed that reception camps would in reality be closed camps and as a consequence unlawful.

Inhuman treatment

It should be noted that a breach of Article 3 of the European Convention on Human Rights (ECHR) is likely since it states that "no one shall be subjected to torture or to inhuman or degrading treatment or punishment". Here, it must be added that this estimation can only be provisional since the real conditions cannot be foreseen. Anyway, it is very possible that inhuman treatment will arise in such centres or even during the removal of an asylum seeker, because it is not indicated that UNHCR standards concerning the detention of asylum seekers would be given. Besides, it is very probable that the claimant does not have any "legal representation or access to a court of law and will have neither the time nor the facilities to make the necessary preparations to support their applications for asylum". Another critical point is the fact of being hosted in closed camps and the additional burden of being far away from those family members that are already in the envisaged EU Member State (Finch / MacDonald 2003: §32-35).

Amnesty International affirms that inhuman treatment is very likely to occur. In its opinion, it may especially take place during forced transfer to the reception camps. This statement is based on the high number of known human rights abuses connected to forced returns (Amnesty International 2003: 21).

Summarising the abovementioned estimations, inhuman treatment seems to be a product of extra-territorial processing. Hence, a further breach of international law may be identified.

Discrimination

The Geneva Refugee Convention demands in its preamble that "human beings shall enjoy fundamental rights and freedoms without discrimination" (UNHCR 1996:15). In other words, it is stipulated that the obligations under the Convention are not perceived selectively. But dividing asylum seekers into different categories with the consequence of different treatment would represent a certain kind of discrimination and would in order be unlawful (Amnesty International 2003: 19). In the case of the UK proposal the discrimination would be based on the fact of arriving in the UK as an asylum seeker while the UNHCR discriminates on the basis of nationality (Amnesty International 2003: 23).

Furthermore, the states tend to discriminate the "onward movers", in contrary to the "good refugees" who stay in the camps. The reason for this discrimination may be found in the supposition that onward movers must be economic migrants. If they were "real refugees" they would be satisfied with living in camps. Amnesty International considers that "it is unfair to condemn those who try actively to find protection rather than waiting for protection to come to them" (Amnesty International 2003: 33). Anyhow, if asylum seekers get different protection depending on their nationality, this is very likely to contravene international law by representing a form of discrimination (Noll 2003: 27).

The discriminating aspect seems to be a further unlawful characteristic of the UNHCR proposal as well as the UK proposal. It is therefore very likely that another incompatibility with international law is existent.

Common rules across the EU

Another critic point is the fact that the proposals do not specify the legal regime. In contrast, they assume existing common rules across the EU. The EU Committee of the House of Lords does not believe that those rules required will be established in the near future since the Member States needed four years to finally agree just on minimum standards on asylum procedures (House of Lords 2004: 30, § 81). Besides, collective responsibility might lead to a variety of problems. If responsibility was moved from the national to the EU level, responsibility would be a collective one. The Immigration Law Practitioners' Association (ILPA) fears that collective responsibility for asylum "is something that is very difficult to make accountable in international law terms". Furthermore, the House of Lords does not even see an "adequate justification for a radical transfer of responsibility" (House of Lords 2004: 30–31, § 83–84).

Common rules across the EU will be very difficult to create and even more difficult to handle. This aspect does not break international law but may be used as a further argumentation that processing is legally unfeasible.

Collective Expulsion

In the Danish Memorandum it is suggested that certain groups may be admitted to protection zones en bloc. Gregor Noll asks if as a consequence group rejections could become reality as well. If yes how should that be determined (Noll 2003: 16). A group rejection would signify a breach of Art. 14(1) of the Universal Declaration on Human Rights that demands the right for everybody to seek asylum. A group determination procedure for example on the basis of nationality could never be compatible with this article. Concerning the resettlement agreements, a group determination would also mean that a whole group shall be resettled. If any state has "the fiscal muscle and the political will to bring either numbers or resettle numbers up to that level" is doubtful (Noll 2003: 17).

In conclusion, the authors of the proposals "have failed to analyse the lawfulness of the schemes" as Amnesty International puts it (Amnesty International 2003:19). According to the legal analysis above, it is extremely probable that the realisation of the externalisation plans would lead to the breach of a variety of international norms. Even if the 1951 Geneva Convention was amended as proposed by the UK, the incompatibility with international law would still exist. And even if we suppose that processing outside the application country is legally possible as long as it is done in a safe country, the transfer of responsibility, inhuman treatment in closed camps and discrimination highly decrease the feasibility of extra-territorial processing. To conclude, externalisation is no adequate instrument from a legal point of view.

4.2.3 Would the principle of international solidarity be fulfilled?

This question seems to be very important because international solidarity is one of the main aims of the international community. It is used as argumentation in a variety of circumstances, but difficult to explain. Therefore, first of all, the concept of international solidarity shall be explained.

What exactly is international solidarity?

A detailed definition of the principle of international solidarity does not exist. That is probably the reason why it is often the subject of discussions as for example at the 49th and the 53rd session of the UNHCR Executive Committee (Catz et al. 2003: 31). Solidarity usually means the alliance of single parts to an integral whole. In the international context, this signifies mutual help between the countries in times of crisis. Concerning the asylum problem, the Preamble of the 1951 Geneva Convention would describe the principle of international solidarity as follows: "(...) the grant of asylum may place unduly heavy burdens on certain countries(...). Satisfactory solution of a problem of which the United Nations has recognized the international scope and nature cannot therefore be achieved without international cooperation" (UNHCR 1996: 15). In other words, the Convention Signatory States obliged themselves to cooperation in case of 'unduly heavy burdens' on a specific country. On the occasion of the 50th anniversary of the Geneva Convention, thus in 2001, the Signatory States even strengthened the importance of international solidarity by signing a further Declaration[34]. There it is emphasised that protection for refugees shall be "enhanced through committed international cooperation in a spirit of solidarity and effective responsibility and burden-sharing among all states" (Catz et al. 2003: 31). I would evaluate this part of the Declaration as an enlargement of the above mentioned cited element of the Geneva Convention. The prerequisite for international cooperation in the latter are 'unduly heavy burdens' that obviously need to be "proved" afterwards which needs additional energy and time to do so. In contrast, the Declaration may be interpreted as the installation of burden-sharing mechanisms beforehand. That is, in my opinion, a great easing in quality since, if such mechanisms will be realised, they would relieve the heavenly burdened countries from the first day on. Even more surprising then that several EU ministers currently support the idea of extra-territorial processing as it may be estimated a burden shifting towards poorer countries.

Externalisation in the context of international solidarity

Some would obviously see a breach of the principle of international solidarity since externalised reception camps are "ghettoes created by the world's most peaceful and richest countries in some of the world's poorest und most unstable regions". Moreover, sending back people to developing countries would mean an additional burden to those parts of the world that already host 72% of the world refugees (Prasad 2003). ECRE shares this opinion (ECRE 2003). Furthermore, Amnesty International criticizes the UK's Transit Processing Centres. "The real goal behind the UK proposal appears to be to reduce the numbers of spontaneous arrivals in the UK and other EU states by denying access to territory and shifting asylum-seekers to zones outside the EU where refugee protection would be weak and unclear", an Amnesty International spokesman comments (Travis 2003). The non-conformity with the principle of international solidarity seems to be a very important argument since externalisation would signify burden shifting towards poorer countries. It might be argued that the externalised centres would be financed by the EU and the use of non-EU territory would probably be highly compensated by payments, hence burden shifting is not the case. It is doubtful if compensation payments

[34] Declaration of States Parties to the 1951 Geneva Convention and the 1967 Protocol

alone correspond to the principle of international solidarity. Gregor Noll[35] would definitely say that its correspondence is "insufficient" (Catz et al. 2003: 31). ECRE and USCR even state that there is no reason why countries with processing capacity should not offer asylum procedures (Catz et al. 2003: 46). All in all, the compatibility of international solidarity and the externalisation proposals is highly doubtful. The UNHCR, however, expresses the will to continue to work on those ideas with the European Commission and the Member States (Travis 2003).

4.2.4 Resources – comprehensively elaborated and realistic?

Envisaged financial resources are not concretely presented in the proposals, but it is claimed in the UK proposal that extra-territorial processing will be financed by the savings of the decreasing number of spontaneous arrivals. In contrast to that, different sources estimate that externalisation would for sure contribute to cost increase even if the UK argues in a different way. The UK supposes that an externalisation will lead to savings since it would result in a reduction of the spontaneous arrivals. Those savings could be used for financing a better protection. Gregor Noll judges that this belief is "based on a blend of plan economy with a dose of science fiction" (Noll 2003: 20). The EU Committee of the House of Lords agrees for the following reasons. The realisation of reception centres would imply that a majority of asylum seekers would be removed two times. First, they would be automatically transferred to the centre, then, they would need to be either sent back to a Member State or to the region of origin. No matter if asylum is granted or not, a system like that would cost a lot of money (House of Lords 2004: 31:§ 86). It must be noted here that – depending on the proposal – not all categories are automatically brought to a centre and thus, the transfer costs do not arise for them. Nevertheless, the costs for procedures that find out to which category of asylum seeker a person belongs to must be considered. In the case of asylum seekers belonging to those categories whose asylum procedures are externalised, those costs must be calculated in addition to the double-transfer costs (House of Lords 2004: 31:§86). Gregor Noll describes those supplementary costs as the following:

First of all, there are the costs connected to the region of origin's will to sign readmission agreements and to the host country's will to install reception centres. Experiences tell us that these costs are very high. Australia, for example, paid 1 million AUD[36] (Australian Dollar) to Papua

[35] Gregor Noll (1998) "On the record", OTR UNHCR Vol.2, Iss. 4, part 2, October 1998.
[36] On the 12th of May, one AUD equalled 0,53 Euro.

New Guinea and 20 million AUD to Nauru in the Fiscal year 2001/02 just so that the governments agreed on Reception camps on their territory. Furthermore, there are costs that also arise in centres inside the EU such as for the provision of human rights, the management of the camp and the initial screening of spontaneous arrivals. Security costs and those of detention are more expensive in the externalised case as is confirmed by the Australian example. Detaining an asylum seeker on Christmas Island is more expensive than on the Australian mainland. It costs almost three times as much as at Woomera and more than three times as much as at Port Hedland. Auxiliary costs come up from the double-transfers as stated above. Noll adds here that they will even be higher if the transfers are involuntary. Besides, the remuneration of the "expatriate expert staff" needs to be considered. Finally, supposing that extra-territorial processing enhances illegal immigration, it is very important to try to add the connected costs for society, even if they are difficult to value (Noll 2003: 20–22).

To show that the externalisation is a very expensive idea, the Australian budget for the fiscal years from 2002/03 to 2005/06 shall be examined[37]. In the Sidney Morning Herald, the budget for those years was presented. The savings of externalised processing by reducing the number of cases processed on Australian mainland are estimated at $85.8 million in 2002/03, $86.9 million in 2003/04, $88 million in 2004/05, and $89.3 million in 2005/06. These savings are due to fewer expenses for detention and processing on the mainland and may be used to finance the extra-territorial processing. The expenses for reception and processing on Australian territory other than the mainland are as follows: in 2002/3 – $81.9 million, in 2003/4 – $122.8 million, in 2004/5 – $ 124.4 million, and in 2005/6 – $ 126.0 million. The reception and processing outside the Australian territory will arise to $129.3 million in 2002/3, $99.3 million in 2003/4, $100.5 million in 2004/5 and $101.7 million in 2005/6. According to Kingston, there are another $300 million to pay for dissuading refugees to do the journey. In the fiscal year 2001/02, the Australian government planned to welcome 5500 illegal boat people on the mainland. For the fiscal year 2002/03, the number shall be reduced to 4500 boat people in outside territory. To prevent one refugee arriving costs $300 000, which, supposing the reduction in the arrivals is 1000 – leads to extra costs of $300 million. The expenses clearly exceed the savings, which will lead to a net loss of $835,9 million in the fiscal years 2002/03 to 2005/06 (Kingston 2002).

---

[37] For more detailed information on Australian budget see http://www.budget.gov.au [accessed 21 April 2005].

Figure 2: The Australian budget for the fiscal years from 2002/03 to 2005/06, data from Kingston 2002

(in million $)	2002/03	2003/04	2004/05	2005/06	Sum
Savings from the offshore processing strategy	85,8	86,9	88	89,3	350
Reception/processing in Australian external territories	81,9	122,8	124,4	126	455,1
Reception/processing in third countries	129,3	99,3	100,5	101,7	430,8
	-125,4	-135,2	-136,9	-138,4	-535,9
Dissuasion of journeys					-300
					-835,9

These results are of great importance since some saving assumptions in the Danish Memorandum are based on the Australian example. In other words, the reduction of numbers of spontaneous arrivals will compensate for the costs of extra-territorial processing and in the end lead to "a decrease in related costs. (...) The cost per capita might initially appear disproportionate, but should be viewed in conjunction with the saving generated in the medium and long term."[38] Noll doubts if the Australian experiences were studied in detail (Noll 2003: 19). Comparing these statements to the results of the Australian budget, I would share Noll's doubts.

Summarising the experiences from Australia and the experts' estimation, extra-territorial processing would certainly lead to an increase in financial costs. Tony Blair's claim of decreasing costs may not be confirmed here since the resource examination concerns financial costs. If we apply economic theory and enlarge the definition of costs to political and social ones, the picture may change under certain circumstances as will be shown in Chapter 4.3. However, the financial costs of externalisation will be very high, but are not comprehensively elaborated in the proposals.

4.2.5 Is the externalisation idea politically useable?

The degree of political usability of a (potential) measure describes up to what extend measures are apt at improving/damaging the elections' results. The higher the political usability of a proposition, hence the higher its positive effect on the success of the initiating party on election day, and

[38] Danish Memorandum 2003, p 4 and p 6, adopted from Noll 2003, p 19.

in turn the higher the probability of a party realising a particular idea. In democracies, politicians will orientate their offers to the voter's demand, or as Matthew J. Gibney puts it for asylum policies: "In democratic states, the costs that any government will be willing to bear for refugees and asylum seekers will be greatly affected by public attitudes" (Gibney 2004: 244). Hence, the realisation of an idea is a lot more probable if it will satisfy and be well accepted by the envisaged section of the electorate. To find out if externalised reception camps as a Common EU Asylum Policy are feasible, we need to look at its political usability. Therefore, we need to ask if a majority of the EU citizens would like the idea of extra-territorial processing. It may be estimated that externalisation meets the desires of a large number of EU citizens. This claim is based on a double branch explanation attempt. The economic theory offers the NIMBY-principle that explains generally why people would vote for externalisation. The second part strongly confirms the applicability of the NIMBY principle in times of anxiety and terrorism. But first we need to define this principle.

What is the NIMBY principle?

NIMBY stands for "not in my backyard" and is observed as a phenomenon in connection to desirable projects for societies. The members of a society are conscious about the necessity of waste incinerators, prisons and nuclear power plants, but are not willing to bear the burden of hosting such facilities as a single neighbourhood or community for the whole society. In other words, the installation of such facilities would signify costs for those members living close to them, while all members of the society may enjoy the benefits. Economically speaking, the support for NIMBY-projects is strong because it is seen as being a public good (Frey 2001: 73). As a consequence, everybody sees that they will profit from the realisation of the project externalisation, and do not bear the costs. Free-riding is the best alternative.

The economic theory offers a solution to the NIMBY-phenomenon. "As the aggregated net benefits of undertaking the projects are positive, one must simply redistribute them in an appropriate way." The ones bearing the costs need to be compensated so that the net benefit is positive, while the others need to be taxed to finance the compensation (Frey 1997: 68). Such an outcome might be reached by using auction mechanisms that might be more or less complex. Just to understand the idea behind it, the most simple compensation auction mechanism with sealed bids is briefly explained here.

A state wants to install a prison, but cannot find a host for it. Then the auction mechanism could lead to a result. Every community of the state would need to lay down the minimum amount of money required to be ready to host a NIMBY facility without knowing the bids of the other communities. The one with the lowest bid is the "winner" of the auction and, as a consequence, the future host of the facility in question. To compensate the host community, the other communities need to pay a share in relation to their bids. A high initial bid also signifies a large share of compensation payments (Quah/Tan 1998: 260-262).

Externalisation in the context of the NIMBY principle

Proceeding on the assumption that the society is the EU (instead of a state) and it needs to install a reception camp where centralised processing and resulting distribution shall be done as the UNHCR proposes. In the case of the EU, the selection of a host can be based on states, regions or communities – this does not really change anything. But since a state basis would signify that the state itself needs to find a host community, it is probably less complex to adjust the auction mechanism to communities. If everyone thinks that it is necessary, but it should not be realised in "her or his backyard", the project is passed on like a hot potato until it arrives outside the EU. As mentioned above, the motivation to be the host community of such a camp is expressed in the willingness-to-pay. If the benefits of a project are exceeded by the costs or vice versa largely depends on the community's perception. Benefits may be brought through the satisfaction of altruistic motives, while costs do not only mean financial costs, but also political and social costs, as carried out in Chapter two.

The perception itself might be highly influenced by the community's wealth. In connection to the auction mechanism, this would mean that a state with high net marginal perceived costs and enough financial resources would certainly bid at a high level, while poorer countries could not afford to do so. The price, which is in this case the bid, would reveal the real preferences of each state. What does that mean for our EU example? The UNHCR proposal probably supposed that the welfare level in the EU 15 is higher than in the new EU Member States. As a consequence, the acceptance of a reception camp is more likely in a new than in an old EU Member State. That is exactly what the UNHCR suggested. If the legal and practical possibility of a further pushing away was given, the population is supposed to make use of it. Even if the financial costs may not be decreased, declines in the political and social costs are ensured. Therefore, assuming the existence of the NIMBY phenomenon, extra-territorial processing is very likely to be the most broadly accepted alternative.

The framing theory confirms the existence of the NIMBY-frame also in the context of asylum seekers and goes even further: Since it is difficult to find moral arguments against asylum centres, refusal is hardly justifiable. "The frame stimulates people to search for (specious) arguments justifying why one has to be against" it (Van Gorp 2001: 10-11). Such an argument may be the already discussed security aspect. Otto Schily gives good reason for externalisation by emphasising the necessity to decrease the deaths on the Mediterranean Sea. Thus, people who do not want asylum seekers in their backyard may argue with the necessity of enhancing the security of potential refugees.

However, the economic theory uses the NIMBY phenomenon to explain the refusal of projects that are necessary for society, but costly for the host community. In the case of asylum centres, politicians have found an ideal solution to the NIMBY phenomenon by outsourcing it. On the one hand, outsourcing still enables them to satisfy the altruistic motives of a large number of EU citizens by knowing that the EU is taking care of asylum seekers. It is not important where this is done, but that it is done. Or, as Timothy J. Hatton (2004: 46) puts it: "(...) individuals might be expected to obtain some benefit from the knowledge that refugees also find safety in countries other than their own." On the other hand, in the case of externalisation, it would not be done in the backyard of any of the EU citizens. These two aspects speak for the potential political popularity of outsourcing the asylum matter and would leave "extraterritorial burden shifting as amongst the only politically 'feasible' strategies" (Betts 2004:67). Hence, the economic theory gives an explanation for the emergence and the political usability of the externalisation idea by applying the NIMBY principle to the asylum matter.

It's a good time for it

The existence of the NIMBY phenomenon in principal is enforced by the current political circumstances. The terrorist attacks in the Western world and the connected increase in anxiety leads to "less tolerant" states (Gibney 2002: 42), or as James Milner (2000: 2) puts it: "(...) asylum will become increasingly scarce in countries where hosting refugees is perceived to be a threat to state security." Due to the perceived threat of terrorist attacks in the Western world, asylum legislation became more restrictive and an asylum seeker "is increasingly viewed as a vehicle through which terrorists and other undesirables might enter Western states" (Gibney 2002: 40; Statewatch June 2003). Therefore, a large number of people would vote for the outsourcing of asylum.

Empirical evidence for the desire of a more restrictive asylum policy is evident from data from a survey made by "market" in 2005, an Austrian opinion research institute. In Austria, 63% of the population want less tolerance in asylum matters[39]. That shows that at least in Austria the idea of an externalised reception camp for asylum seekers may fall back on a majority and has a great political usability. Within the EU, a similar attitude may be observed in a variety of countries. The "Eurobarometer" based on field study in December 2003 and published in March 2004 dealt among others with the following hypothesis: "Controls of entry into the European Union for persons coming from non-Member States should be strengthened". The externalised asylum procedure would represent a strengthening of the entry control with the aim to open the borders of the EU only for "genuine refugees. In all of the 15 "old" Member States more than 40% absolutely agree with the above-mentioned statement. In Austria, Finland, the Netherlands and Portugal it is more then 50%, and in Germany, Greece, Italy and Luxembourg it is even more than 60% that absolutely agree with it[40]. Timothy J. Hatton (2004) confirms that "the majority opinion is that immigration should be reduced". Interestingly, there seems to be even more hostility against asylum seekers and refugees than against other immigrants (Hatton 2004: 44). From these results it may be concluded that the externalisation idea would correspond to the views of a majority of people and thus have a great political usability.

The existing political usability may also be confirmed by referring to the Australian experience of its "South Pacific Solution". Restrictions in asylum policy by realising externalised refugee reception camps were strongly supported by public opinion. 77% of Australians were for the government's policy. The elections two months later, in November 2001, were further proof of the electoral enhancing effect of asylum externalisation. The Howard government finally won the elections even though, before the Tampa crisis, it had very bad results in opinion polls (Gibney 2004: 189). These facts as well as the abovementioned empirical evi-

---

[39] Data available at: http://www.networld.at/index.html?/articles/0419/10/81234.shtml [accessed 16 September 2005].

[40] This Flash-Eurobarometer nr. 155 was requested by Directorate General Justice and Home Affairs and realised by EOS Gallup Europe between 8 December 2003 and 16 December 2003. The report on it is available at: http://europa.eu.int/comm/public_opinion/flash/fl155_report_en.pdf [accessed 17 Sept. 2005].

dence show that more restrictive asylum policies like externalisation would be of high political usability because a large majority of the electorate "simply are intolerant" concerning economic migrants taking the asylum channel or taking advantage of poor border controls (Gibney 2004: 245).

The political usability of an externalised solution to the asylum problems seems to be very high. Timothy J. Hatton estimates that the public and political opinion strongly exceeds the influence of economic costs and benefits that only have modest effects (Hatton 2004: 44). Provided that this is true, the high degree of political usability, hence the very probable support by EU citizens, could have a strong positive impact on the realisation of externalised EU reception camps.

4.2.6 Is extra-territorial processing feasible?

The analysis results in a variety of counter-arguments to externalisation. Externalised reception camps do not seem to be an adequate way to reach the objectives. Neither the limiting aspect nor the security aspect would be achieved. Furthermore, potential risks are not considered, certain parts are unlawful, the principle of international solidarity is not fulfilled and it would signify a further financial burden for the EU Member States. All these aspects speak against the realisation of common reception camps outside the EU. Or, as the IGC (1995: 7 in Noll 2003: 9) puts it: "(...) the 'exclusive' option is not feasible and as such, does not deserve further elaboration". But there is still its high political usability. In times of terrorist attacks, a majority of EU citizens would prefer to close the borders to protect Europe from foreign influences and potential terrorists. In other words, the majority of the electorate would vote for the party that takes on the will of the citizens.

Since in democracies parties depend on majorities, the political aspect of externalised EU reception camps should not be neglected. It is obvious that politicians will need to offer answers to the voter's fear – either by confirming it through more restrictive laws or by trying to influence the voter's perception of refugees. The first option seems to be more probable in the short term. The politicians "believe that ever more restrictive measures will eliminate public discontent. And, in the short term, they may well be right. But, in the longer term, a better way (...) might be by increasing people's sense of the moral value of the institution of asylum" (Gibney 2004: 245). Since democracies offer elections every four years, the politicians' short-term view might be estimated to be more important than their long-term view. Therefore, more restrictions in asylum jurisdiction seem to be very likely in the near future. Regarding its political usability, the feasibility of externalised reception camps is increasing. Nevertheless, the abovementioned obstacles cannot be neglected.

We return to the original question of this paper. Would common EU reception camps outside the EU represent an adequate burden sharing system? As we have seen it is not adequate for legal and humanitarian reasons, but it is adequate for political reasons. To be able to give a comprehensive answer, we need to look at externalisation aiming at a more efficient or a more equitable burden sharing. To incorporate efficiency seems to be important since especially the UK proposal used the efficiency argument to justify externalisation. But what does efficiency mean? What is a "more efficient burden sharing system"? The next chapter calls in the economic theory that offers different efficiency concepts to examine if externalisation could lead to a more efficient burden sharing system. In a further step, externalisation will also be looked at from the perspective of equity.

4.3 Efficiency versus equity – an economic qualitative analysis

The main question of this paper takes up the adequacy of externalised reception camps in the context of burden sharing. As mentioned in Chapter two, the burden sharing debate focused for a long time on a more equitable system (Suhrke 1998: 398). Either an EU wide policy harmonisation or a quota setting could reach this aim. The difficulty of the first option is the risk of a harmonised EU asylum system on a very low level due to the lack of the willingness to compromise the EU Member States (Hatton 2004: 51). A decisive advantage however is that the refugees do not need to be physically transferred (Suhrke 1998: 412). The quota solution, on the other hand, aims towards equity in a stricter form than harmonised policies. In a quota setting the burden of asylum seekers is distributed among the states depending on for example its size and its Gross National Product. Hence, each state carries the burden that corresponds to its power. Quotas could signify state specific financial contributions like for the European Refugee Fund (Thielemann 2005: 15-17). In this case, physical transfer of refugees is not required. Nevertheless, a burden sharing system aiming at more equity could imply that refugees need to be physically transferred. In other words, refugees are sent to a country depending on a certain distribution key, which Germany had proposed in its 1994 draft resolution (Suhrke 1998: 410). However, regardless of a physical transfer or not, all these burden sharing instruments head towards a more equitable distribution without looking at its efficiency. But, in the last couple of years and especially in the UK proposal, the aim of a more efficient burden sharing was emphasised – up to now only on a theoretical basis.

But why shall it be more efficient? Looking at the post-war period as done in Chapter two, we may discover that the prerequisites for a voluntary burden sharing correspond to rational behaviour. States will more probably agree on burden sharing if they can benefit from it as they did because of the increased labour demand in the post war boom. Thielemann (2005: 12-14) also talks about interest based motivations to be stronger than norm based motivations (Chapter two). The latter can be derived from the principle of international solidarity. Interest based motivations could appear as follows: states agree on burden sharing because they either head towards a "refugee crisis insurance" in case of mass influx (Schuck 1997: 249), or they pursue other objectives, or simply because it is more efficient (Thielemann 2005: 12-14).

We suppose that states would more probably agree on burden sharing in the asylum field if it signified more efficiency. Here, we come very close to environmental economics that have a variety of similarities with asylum. Since environmental economics are a lot more advanced in the efficiency debate, the following chapter will partially fall back on their instruments and experiences. Environmental economics would vote for more efficient instruments since they do not believe in voluntary agreement. Based on the concept of a "homo oeconomicus", individuals will have non-polluting behaviour only if it brings more benefits. Transferring these thoughts on states instead of individuals and the asylum field instead of the environment, we would need a burden sharing system that motivates states to offer protection. In other words, it must be more efficient for states to be part of a burden sharing system than not being part of it. It seems acceptable to draw from individual behaviour to the behaviour of states. New Political Economists and Institutional Economists maintain that political actors are self-interested individuals (Rogall 2002: 113).
The advantages of a more efficient burden sharing system is that asylum would be less connected to incredibly high costs since it "is likely to reduce the costs associated with the humanitarian principle through gains associated with greater efficiencies" (Gibney 2004: 246).

We have however already examined the aims of EU reception camps and its legal, humanitarian and political consequences to be able to determine its adequacy. Finally, we want to examine externalised asylum solutions on its adequacy as a burden sharing system. As we know, a burden sharing mechanism may head towards different aims – either more efficiency or more equity.

This last chapter will treat the question which aim is reached under which circumstances by EU reception camps – or, in other words, if an externalised solution is an instrument which reaches more equity or more efficiency. The analysis in turn will take the respective aim as given. Thus, it will not investigate the ideologically influenced decision process for one aim or the other even if it would be highly interesting to look at it because of its comprehensive consequences. Samuelson and Nordhaus (1995: 141) consider it to be "one of the most profound questions of value that a society faces". Nevertheless, this work keeps it like Barr (1998: 98): "The proper place of ideology is in the choice of aims (...) but once these aims have been agreed, the choice of method should be regarded as a technical issue rather than an ideological one".

A qualitative analysis

The analysis of EU reception camps as a more efficient or more equitable burden sharing system will be based on an economic qualitative analysis frame proposed by Joseph E. Stiglitz and Bruno Schönfelder (1989: 236-255). This frame seems to be very useful for our purpose since it aims at the examination of the efficiency and the equity of a measure. Initially, it asks if and why state intervention is necessary. Then, it looks at its efficiency and equity consequences. Finally, the political decision process shall be examined (Stiglitz/Schönfelder 1989). This paper especially emphasises the efficiency criterion since, on the one hand, it is explicitly mentioned in the UK proposal, and, on the other hand, it is the aim that is currently emphasised within the burden sharing debate.

4.3.1 Necessity of state intervention – does market failure occur?

Welfare economics[41] suggest a market to be efficient as long as it fulfils a variety of standard assumptions. These are perfect competition, complete markets, the absence of market failures, and perfect information. Where all these assumptions are accomplished, state intervention for

[41] Welfare economics is a branch of economics that simultaneously uses microeconomic techniques to determine the allocative efficiency of a macroeconomy and the income distribution consequences associated with it. It attempts to maximize the level of social welfare by examining the economic activities of the individuals that comprise society. For further details: http://en.wikipedia.org/wiki/Welfare_economics [accesed 14 October 2005].

reasons of efficiency is not justified. But as soon as one of these is not given, state intervention is legitimate (Barr 1998: 78).

What is market failure?

Market failure describes the "situation in which an unregulated competitive market is inefficient because prices fail to provide proper signals to consumers and producers" (Pyndick/Rubinfeld 2001: 294). It occurs in the case of market power (when monopolies may influence prices), incomplete information (in case of a lack of correct information on the consumer side), external effects and public goods (Pyndick et al. 2001: 592-594).
Assuming the asylum provision to be our good, externalities and public goods are of our interest. What do these effects describe? External effects occur when the production or consumption of a good affects a third person. This may either be negative, hence imposing costs on a third party, or positive, imposing benefits on the third. However, these external costs or benefits are not reflected in the market price which leads to sub-optimal production. Either, in the case of negative externalities, the production is too high, or, in the case of positive externalities, the production is too low to be efficient. Therefore some kind of intervention is required (Pyndick/Rubinfeld 2001: 621-623). Public goods are goods that are characterised by non-excludability and non-rivalry. The first means that "the marginal cost of providing it to an additional consumer is zero". An example may be a highway in times of low traffic. An additional driver would not lead to more costs. That leads us to the second characteristic – the non-excludability. That signifies that no one can be excluded from consuming it or exclusion would not make any sense (Pyndick/Rubinfeld 2001: 644-645). Paul Samuelson and William Nordhaus (1995) explain it in a way that is easier to understand.

> *Public goods are ones whose benefits are invisibly spread among the entire community, whether or not individuals desire to purchase the public good. Private goods, by contrast, are ones that can be divided up and provided separately to different individuals, with no external benefits or costs to others. Efficient provision of public goods often requires government action, while private goods can be efficiently allocated by markets (Samuelson/Nordhaus 1995: 347).*

Another example of a public good would be national defence. As soon as it is provided, everybody must "consume" security (which represents – at least for the majority of people a positive externality). Furthermore, the costs for its "production" remain the same, independent from the number of "consumers". In contrast, a typical private good is bread. One kilogram of bread may be consumed by one person or by ten persons. Hence, the distribution of this one kilogram of bread may take a variety of different forms. Nevertheless, as soon as it is eaten, it is not available anymore for other individuals (Samuelson/Nordhaus 1995: 347).

In the above mentioned cases, market failure exists, and, the market outcome is not efficient and state intervention into the market is therefore justified. The terminus of "state intervention" may also be used for the intervention of the EU since it gradually becomes – at least in some policy fields – similar to a federal state. In the following chapter, talking about state intervention always refers to the intervention of the EU. Anyhow, to look at the necessity of state intervention, we need to ask whether one of these cases fit into the asylum field. As already mentioned, the two effects of our interest are public goods and external effects.

What kind of good refers to asylum?

This paper assumes that our good is security. An asylum seeker receives the good security if granted asylum to an EU member state. It seems acceptable to claim that security will be enhanced, because asylum is only granted to persons who would be exposed to insecurity in their home countries. Therefore, living within the EU would signify more security for them. It is a private good since it is characterised by rivalry and excludability. As the last couple of years have shown, the increasing number of asylum seekers led to restrictions in the asylum policies within the EU, with the result that it has become much more difficult to get asylum. Matthew Gibney (2004) also estimates that asylum is a scarce good. Offering asylum to for instance family members of recognized refugees would "limit the ability of the state to accept refugees" (Gibney 2004: 250). This statement emphasises that there is rivalry in the consumption of asylum.

For our analysis, however, it is more important to investigate the EU perspective. We assume that security would be a public good within the EU, either producing positive or negative externalities. Supposing an asylum system with severe legal immigration possibilities, less people would need to arrive to the EU illegally. It may be assumed that less illegal persons would signify more security. In other words, providing legal immigration possibilities would lead to positive externalities in the sense that nobody could be excluded from the enhanced security. But legal immigration possibilities to the EU hardly exist and therefore, positive externalities do not correspond to reality. It might be assumed that the assumption of negative externalities is more realistic. A lot of people feel less secure because of the presence of asylum seekers. As broadly discussed in 4.2.5, media often strengthen such feelings by emphasising criminal acts of asylum seekers in detail or foreigners in general. Thus, it seems acceptable to assume that the provision of asylum is a public good with negative externalities – perceived at least by a majority of EU citizens. This definition corresponds to the pure public good model.

The economic literature offers a variety of discussions about the question which kind of good the provision of asylum is. This discussion will be reproduced further down in the context of the efficiency debate (4.3.2).

Does market failure occur?

Synthesising the initially presented theory with the assumed existence of public goods and negative externalities, this paper diagnoses market failure and, as a consequence, the justification of state intervention. If this was not given, state intervention would not be justified and the forthcoming analysis would not make any sense. But since this is not the case, it is legitimate that politicians and experts are looking for measures to improve the asylum system. The examination on the measure of externalisation may continue.

4.3.2 Externalisation - a more efficient burden sharing mechanism?

Incorporating externalisation into the burden sharing debate signifies a very new quality. Up to that moment, the only way of burden sharing was financial compensation (via the European Refugee Fund). Contrary to the pure transfer of money, externalisation would signify a physical transfer of refugees. This has two significant consequences. Since the concerned costs are not anymore only of financial nature, the cost term may be extended to social and political costs as it was done in Chapter two. Second, the concept of efficiency may be incorporated more easily. Especially the UK proposal uses the term of "a more efficient burden sharing" as a goal, but does not define it further. As long as a clear definition lacks, the aim of more efficiency does not have any meaningfulness, or as Alexander Betts (2005: 32) writes, it "will either favour arbitrary outcomes or privilege the interests of those that use it as a legitimation tool". Therefore, to examine whether externalisation would be an efficient burden sharing system, a variety of fixings would need to be done. To do so, this paper will develop the questions that Alexander Betts asked in the conclusion of a working paper realised for the University of Oxford in 2005. Accordingly, the following questions must be answered before even being capable to examine if efficiency would be reached by externalised reception camps.

- *Question 1:*
  What kind of good is protection?
- *Question 2:*
  Does the cost term only imply monetary costs or also perceived costs?
- *Question 3:*
  More efficiency for the EU Member States, the international community or refugees? Who would profit from it?
- *Question 4:*
  Does the aim of more efficiency refer to productive or allocative efficiency, and to a static or a dynamic approach?

(Betts 2005: 31)

To be able to answer these questions, the above mentioned terms need to be explained and defined. Finally, the paper will be able to answer the question under which conditions the external solution would create more efficiency than the current asylum systems in the EU Member States.

4.3.2.1 What kind of good is protection?

As mentioned above, this paper assumes protection, hence security, to be a public good at least for EU citizens. A variety of authors confirm the characteristics of a public good, namely, non-excludability and rivalry (Suhrke 1998: 399, Hatton 2004: 46) which are non-excludability and non-rivalry. Note that these characteristics usually lead to free-riding and therefore risk a sub-optimal provision of public goods. If sub-optimality is mentioned in this chapter, it describes economic inefficiency, but does not refer to the amount of asylum provision that would be morally desirable. Hence, the sub-optimal provision of asylum results in an inefficient output. The public good theory therefore suggests intervening measures to optimise the outcome (Barbou des Places/Deffains 2003: 5). In this context, Olson and Zeckhauser (1966, cited by Barbou des Places/Deffain 2005: 6) advance the "exploitation hypothesis" saying that large countries are exploited by small countries. Since their contribution to the provision of public goods will have a lot more weight, they are more motivated to participate in the burden sharing disproportionately. An example may underpin this statement. In several articles it is said that the Western Alliance produces a sup-optimal outcome of its good which is military security. The reason is that most countries are free-riding on the United States' contributions to military security. That means that the big is exploited by the small. Nevertheless, the United States are motivated to contribute because of their economic weight and their specific geopolitical concerns (Boyer 1989: 701). But, in the case of asylum within the EU, empirical evidence shows the opposite – small EU Member States investing a lot more in the asylum system than their larger neighbours (for details view Chapter two). As a result, the exploitation hypothesis of the public good theory can not be hold. Keith Hartley and Todd Sandler (2001) introduce a "Joint Product Model of Alliances" within the NATO. It seems highly unproblematic to use this model for the produced goods within an asylum system, because in their article it is explicitly indicated that "the joint product model is relevant for virtually every public good scenario" (Hartley/Sandler 2001: 880). The Joint Product model is based on a model by van Ypersele de Strihou (1967, cited by Hartley/Sandler 2001: 876) which introduces the idea of certain ally-specific benefits that may be private. In a footnote, Hartley and Sandler add that even Olson and Zeckhauser already mentioned those specific benefits without further analysing them. However, the joint product model assumes defence "to produce a variety of outputs" – country-specific private goods, impurely and purely public goods (Hartley/Sandler 2001: 876). As mentioned earlier, the model may easily be used for the provision of asylum. In this case, this model says that provision of asylum does not need only to produce public, but also some kind of country-specific private goods. Such a private good may be motivated by altruism. A large number of people and/or countries may derive benefits from knowing that asylum seekers get help in their country (Hatton 2004: 46). If for example Sweden and its population feel so because of their high contribution to the asylum system within the EU, the population of other EU Member States is excluded from these benefits. Hence, the public good characteristic of non-excludability is not given anymore. Such goods may explain why some countries are willing to offer more protection than others. Nevertheless, there are still a variety of public goods that are produced. "Almost any type of security" produces private and public goods (Boyer 1989: 713). Even if the altruistic benefits may be private up to a certain extent, there are still the possible benefits of knowing that other countries are taking care of the poorest, as Hatton (2004: 46) emphasises. To summarise, pure public goods barely exist. It is common that country-specific private goods also occur in this context. But no matter how the division of public and private goods is, "the extent of publicness in the presence of joint products depends on the ratio of excludable benefits to total benefits" (Hartley/Sandler 2001: 876).

The joint product model contradicts the pure public goods theory and hence lessens the statement of sup-optimal provision of asylum because of the free-riding problematic. The more private benefits are produced by the provision of asylum, the weaker the incentives for a country to free-ride since the latter would imply the loss of the private benefits. Or, in other words, "(...) as the percentage of private benefits increase as a percentage of total alliance good production, free-rider tendencies will decrease" (Boyer 1989: 702). As a result, the sub-optimality of the outcome will decrease.

The joint product model seems very realistic in the case of asylum. Readers might ask why the paper used the pure public good model at the beginning if the joint product model is realistic in the case of asylum. It is right that the joint product model may be seen as an enlargement to the pure public good model. But even if asylum might create a variety of private benefits for states, it still leads to the production of international public goods. Thus even if the sub-optimality in provision might decrease, it still exists. And as we know, public goods result in inefficient outcomes that demand state intervention. As the explanation of these connections (legitimating state interventions) was the aim above, this paper wanted to show it by initially only using the pure public good model. But, once again, the paper argues that the joint product model brings a highly important and probably very realistic component into the debate.

4.3.2.2 Monetary and/or perceived costs?

This question was already treated in different parts of the paper and will be summarised here. As the Australian example shows, the monetary costs of external solutions would highly exceed the savings of a decrease in spontaneous arrivals. In other words, only considering monetary costs, externalisation would not represent a more efficient system because it would lead to more costs than needed today. But the picture changes when incorporating perceived costs. As already explained in Chapter 2.1.3.2, these are social and political costs. Social costs[42] arise if the image of asylum seekers is bad. Estimating the majority among them to be

[42] James Milner (2000: 2-3) talks in this context of direct and indirect security burdens of asylum. The former correspond to the risks of conflict spill-over, while the latter refer to the financial and social burdens of asylum seekers on the host country.

criminals, their presence in a country fuels fear and results in increasing social costs. These lead to the rise of the NIMBY ("Not in my backyard") principle (view Chapter 4.2.5) which describes the rejection of socially desirable projects. People know that it is important to take care of asylum seekers, but they do not want to have them in "their backyard". If, concerning asylum, the majority of a society may be characterised through the NIMBY-principle, it would be politically expensive to favour liberal asylum policies. Thus, political costs arise with the loss of public support because of unpopular measures (Betts 2003: 12-15). It is assumed that within a variety of EU Member States, measures are unpopular when in favour of asylum seekers. This assumption is based on the estimation that "ill-considered political pronouncements, hostile expressions of public opinion, and biased media reporting have contributed to the rise of political extremism in some countries, and unease and discrimination in many" (Oxfam 2005: 34).

This paper considers the social and political costs of opening the EU borders to asylum seekers as high and influential. It seems therefore very acceptable to define the cost term in the broad sense of tangible (monetary) and intangible (perceived) costs. This enlargement has a large impact on the efficiency debate in turn. For reasons of easier comprehension, question 3 and questions 4 will be treated at one go.

4.3.2.3 Which efficiency criterion and who would profit from it?

Such an economic theory uses efficiency as a criterion to examine whether the outcome of a measure is optimal. In this context, three criteria with different emphasis may be applied – productive efficiency, allocative efficiency and dynamic efficiency. Only if all three of them are fulfilled, the project is comprehensively efficient and hence, a "first-best" solution. If only one of these criteria is fulfilled, the solution is a "second-best" one. Productive efficiency describes cost-effectiveness regarding a given output. In other words, a project is productively efficient if it is realised at the least costs possible. Allocative efficiency also means Pareto-optimality. Thus, in order to be allocatively efficient, no one's situation may be improved by worsening another one. In economic terms, this is reached in the point where the net benefits are maximised which means where the marginal benefits equal the marginal costs. Hence, an additional unit of consumption brings exactly the same benefit as it arises costs. Both refer to one point in time and may also be summarised as concepts of static efficiency. If time does not play an important rule, the static efficiency criterion may be very useful. But obviously, the occurrence of costs and benefits at different moments needs to be considered. In such cases, the dynamic efficiency criterion may be invoked. It is satisfied by maximising the present value of the net benefits not in comparison to other projects of that period, but over all the periods of interest (Tietenberg 2003: 25-28).

As mentioned before, the burden sharing debate was for a long time characterised by searching for a more equitable distribution of refugees. But in the last couple of years, the objective of efficiency was introduced and, among others, mentioned to argue the necessity of new approaches in the asylum policy. The UK proposal (Blair 2003) denounces that the "support for refugees is badly distributed", because the costs for one asylum seeker are a lot higher in Europe than in other places of the world (10.000$ compared to 50$ per year). In other words, the same level of asylum provision could be reached with fewer costs in another part of the world. This would correspond to productive efficiency which is explained in turn.

Productive efficiency

Productive efficiency is defined as reaching a given output at the least costs. What is the given output? It is a goal that needs to be defined at a certain level. In the asylum case this would be minimal refugee protection. Frequently, the "method" to provide protection is asylum. Obviously, the process of determining minimal protection, based on a certain method, might imply a variety of conflicts. How it is finally defined is a very normative question, but at least, we can limit its definition by stating what it is not. The term of productive efficiency should surely not be used to minimise costs by downgrading the quality of protection. In the contrary, minimum standards need to be respected. Erika Feller, the Director of UNHCR's Department of International Protection, stated at the Fifty-fifth Session of the Executive Committee of the High Commissioner's Programme in Geneva on the 7th of October in 2004 the characteristics of such minimum standards. They "broadly involve avoiding the risk of persecution, refoulement or cruel and degrading treatment; the absence of real risk to life; a genuine prospect of an accessible durable solution; protection against arbitrary expulsion and deprivation of liberty; provision for an adequate and dignified means of subsistence; the unity and integrity of the family is insured; the specific protection needs of the affected persons, including those deriving from age and gender; are able to be identified and respected" (Betts 2005: 9-10). If the given output is the above-mentioned minimum refugee protection, what exactly are the costs arising from it? Protection costs vary among states. Regarding the expenses for legal processing and social security, an asylum seeker yearly costs 16,596 US$ in Denmark, 4,622 US$ in Austria and 348 US$ in Ghana (Jandl 1995, cited by Betts 2005: 10). These numbers only represent financial costs (also called economic, monetary or tangible costs). But, as explained in Chapter two and earlier in this chapter, there are a variety of intangible costs that are not monetarily expressed, but nevertheless very important. Social costs depend on how asylum seekers are perceived. Since the perception of them got worse because of their stigmatisation by media and some politicians, social costs increased especially in the Western world. Related to those perceived costs, liberal asylum policies may be politically costly and are therefore avoided (Betts 2005: 11-12).

Does externalisation correspond to productive efficiency?

Not considering intangible costs would certainly signify that the externalisation of asylum procedures does not reach productive efficiency. Contrary to the assertion in the UK proposal, it may be assumed that the financial costs would strongly increase by realising the externalisation idea. This assumption is based on the experiences of Australia's South Pacific Solution as shown in Chapter 4.2.4. The examination of the data of Australian experience shows how expensive – in terms of financial costs – externalisation projects are. Therefore it is not true that it will finally lead to "a decrease in related costs", as written in the UK proposal. The picture changes if intangible costs are considered. While they grew up to a high level in the last couple of years within the EU (even if there are national differences), there might be other countries in the South where those costs are very low. Externalisation from the EU to countries with low intangible costs would hence lead to the following consequences. As a first step, all costs arising from asylum seekers within the EU would decrease. In the country that hosts the reception camp financial costs would increase while the intangible costs would stay relatively small, because asylum seekers are less seen as a threat as they are in the EU. Obviously, the financial costs of the host country plus further compensation payments would need to be paid by the EU. But it may be argued that even if financial costs increase because of externalisation (as shown above), the intangible costs would decrease.

In this context, the Ricardian theory of comparative advantages shall be mentioned. Mark Boyer (1989) used it as a base for his "New economic theory of alliances that focuses on 'trade' in public goods". It was introduced in the context of providing military security, but will here be used for the provision of asylum.

"The Ricardian theory of comparative advantages"

The Ricardian theory of comparative advantages goes back on David Ricardo who published it in "Principles of Political Economy and Taxation" in 1817 (Mankiw 2001: 55). It mobilises a new perspective to the economic term of an absolute advantage. The latter is used when, for example, a producer needs fewer inputs than another to reach the same output. To state an example, let us assume two producers A and B. Each of them produces meat and potatoes. A needs 8 hours to produce one pound of potatoes, while only one hour for a pound of meat. In contrast, B needs 10 hours for a pound of potatoes and 20 hours for a pound of meat. In both cases, A has an absolute advantage to B. In contrast, the Ricardian comparative advantage does not compare the required inputs, but the connected opportunity costs ("whatever must be given up to obtain the same item"). Let us continue with the above mentioned example. A needs 8 hours to produce a pound of potatoes. During these 8 hours, he or she can not produce meat. Since A only needs one hour for one pound of meat, he or she could produce 8 pounds of meat instead of producing one pound of potatoes. In this case, the opportunity costs for one pound of potatoes are 8 pounds of meat. In contrast, B's opportunity costs for one pound of potatoes would only arise to ½ pound of meat (10 hours for a pound of potatoes, but 20 hours for a pound of meat). As a result, it is obvious that B has a comparative advantage to A in the production of potatoes even if A would have the absolute advantage. An individual may never have a comparative advantage in both goods. Therefore, a specialisation for each of them (A in the production of meat, and B in the production of potatoes) would make sense from an economic point of view. The same output could be reached with fewer costs. Productive efficiency as explained above would be obtained (Mankiw 2001: 53-54).

"New economic theory of alliances"

From the Ricardian theory of the comparative advantage, Mark Boyer (1989) draws his "New economic theory of alliances that focuses on 'trade' in public goods". This theory explains that not only producers specialise, but also countries. So it may be the case that a country free-rides on another country's provision of a certain public good. But, at the same time, the initial free-rider is the one that provides another public good. Mark

Boyer shows this connection by mobilising an international trade model with two countries (country 1 and 2) and two goods (military and economic contributions to obtain security). Each of them might specialise in the production of the good for which it has a comparative advantage. The latter depends on the "national production functions" that are influenced by the "domestic political culture" and the "economic structure". In a democracy, the electorate is quite powerful because of its possibility to vote for or against governments and their measures (Boyer 1989: 704-710). Let us assume that in country 1, civil society is strongly engaged in demonstrations and other actions against war and violence. Introducing military actions might be politically expensive for the government because of a decrease in the probability of being re-elected. Hence, the opportunity costs of military contributions are very high. As a result, country 1 will specialise in economic contributions to security in the form of foreign aid payments. In country 2, however, the production of military goods is highly recognised among the population because it gives the feeling of security, places to work, and welfare. The demand for foreign aid hardly exists. Thus, the opportunity costs for military contributions are lower than in the case of country 1. Therefore, country 2 would come to specialise in the production of military goods.

Boyer (1989) underpins his model by mobilising empirical data of the military expenditures (from 1960 to 1985) and the foreign aid payments (from 1969 to 1985) of the Western Alliance countries. While the United States contributed a high percentage of its Gross Domestic Product to military action, their foreign aid payments are very low. The United States were free-riding on the foreign aid payments of other countries like France, Denmark or the Netherlands (Boyer 1989: 714-722).

The incorporation of the external solution into these theories

Let us apply Boyer's "New economic theory of alliances" on the external solution. In this case, the two parties involved are the EU and, for example, Libya. Based on protection for persecuted people as it is demanded by international law[43], the envisaged aim is a given level of increased security in the meaning of the possibility to seek asylum without being forced to take the dangerous route to the EU. As in Boyer's "New economic theory of alliances", the aim shall be obtained by offering two goods – financial and spatial contributions. The EU could either offer

[43] Article 14.1 of the Universal Declaration of Human Rights or Article 1 of the 1951 Geneva Convention. For further Deteils view 4.2.2.

space in the sense of its soil or pay others do so. The former refers to the creation of legal immigration possibilities, while the second would signify some sort of externalisation. Note that this modelling bases on the assumptions in the different proposals. In contrast, this paper doubts that external reception camps may really lead to increased security on a large scale. Nevertheless, the initial situation shall be reproduced here. However, since the Ricardian theory of comparative advantages is the base, we need to ask for the opportunity costs of for example spatial contributions. As discussed further up, the social and political costs of opening the borders are very high within the EU. In contrast, it is assumed that in Libya these political and social costs exist, but on a smaller scale than in Europe. The exceeding opportunity costs for the EU result in a comparative advantage of spatial contribution for Libya. To check the validity of this outcome, we look at it from the reverse perspective. The opportunity costs of financial contributions arise from not being able to invest in another policy field. Morocco has less financial opportunities than the EU. Therefore, the opportunity costs of using its money for asylum seekers will be higher than for the EU. Hence, the EU has a comparative advantage in the provision of financial resources. In other words, Libya (or any other North African state) makes space available to realise asylum procedures on their soil so that asylum seekers do not need to take the dangerous route to the EU, while the EU would finance it. Up to now, it was assumed that Libya was intrinsically motivated to offer space, but that is very doubtful. Why should Libya take care of asylum seekers whose aim is Europe? Why should Libya offer space to them if they do not even ask to stay? It is very likely that Libya would need extrinsic motivations like financial compensations. This statement may be confirmed by mobilising the Australian "South Pacific Solution". It shows that high compensation payments were required to motivate countries to host the external reception camps (for further details view Chapter 4.2.4). Therefore, it is legitimate to enlarge the model by incorporating "trade" into the debate, or as Boyer (1989: 713) puts it: "(...) combining these implications with the possibilities of trade in public goods provides two strong tendencies towards greater efficiency in alliance good provision".

Going back to the example with the meat and the potato production shows that trade might lead to more efficiency. If the deal was that B gets 3 pounds of meat for 1 pound of potatoes, the price for one pound of meat would be 1/3 of the potato price. If B produced the meat himself or herself, the opportunity costs for one pound of meat would be 2 pound of potatoes. In other words, giving the possibility of trade to B improves his or her situation. The same may be observed for A. He or she may get one pound of potato for 3 pounds of meat. In the case of self-production, his or her

opportunity costs would be 8 pounds of meat. A also profits from the trade relations with B. This example clearly shows that "differences in opportunity costs and comparative advantages create the gains from trade" (Mankiw 2001: 54).
Incorporating a trade component signifies in our model that Libya offers the space for the realisation of asylum procedures because of its comparative advantage to the EU. The latter would "buy" the good "space for asylum processing" by financially compensating Libya. To improve the situation of the EU as well as of Libya, the financial contribution would need to be somewhere between the differing opportunity costs of the two involved parties. The same output could be reached at lower costs. Due to the enlargement of our model by the trade component, it comes closer to the external solution envisaged by the proposals which implies physical transfer of the asylum seekers. In this scenario, the physical transfer of asylum seekers from the EU to external reception camps is considered.

Summarising the above, a given output may be reached at lower costs, if a country specialises on the good where it has a comparative advantage and if trade is possible. Hence, it would be productively more efficient. It is not said that externalisation would lead to the most efficient outcome (productive efficiency is defined as reaching a given output at the lowest costs), because there might be alternatives that even arise less costs. But our question of interest is if externalisation would lead to a more efficient and not to the most efficient burden sharing. Therefore, relying on the above mentioned assumptions and considering intangible costs, externalised reception camps may be called more efficient when efficiency is defined as productive efficiency. But it must be noted that the more efficient output, hence the gains of externalisation, especially refer to the EU. Without externalisation, the EU has to bear all the political and social costs of asylum seekers. Libya would also profit from it, because of the financial compensations. Otherwise, it would never participate in such cooperation. All the rest, especially the asylum seekers, would not profit from it. Even if the given level of security might be reached, this paper assumes that an external solution implies additional costs for asylum seekers on a humanitarian level (view Chapter 4.2). These are not considered in this model.

Allocative efficiency

Allocative efficiency is based on the Pareto-Optimality criterion which is very useful to compare results of different measures. As long as it is possible to improve one's situation without worsen the other's, a Pareto-improvement is still possible. Hence it is Pareto-inefficient. If in applying a certain measure, there is no possibility of a Pareto-improvement, it is Pareto-efficient. To better understand, imagine that a variety of flats are distributed among individuals by coincidence. It may happen that some of them love the country-side, but get a flat in town, while others live in villages, although they would prefer town life. Through barter, people's situation may be improved (because they may exchange flats). When each voluntary barter is realised, thus when all gains of barter are exhausted, we may call an allocation Pareto-efficient (Varian 2001: 14-15). Welfare economics suppose that allocative efficiency is automatically reached in the market, but is not achieved in the case of market failures. As shown further up, market failures exist in the "market" of asylum provision which means that allocative efficiency can not be reached. As in environmental economics, Pigouvian taxes or Coasian property rights solutions could be used to achieve allocative efficiency (Betts 2005: 13). The Pigouvian tax is used "to internalise the negative externality by imposing the full cost on the responsible consumer or producers while compensating the affected third party". In other words, the "free-riders" could compensate those who are overburdened. In this context, the Pigou tax would need to equate the externality to be able to internalise it completely. Obviously, it is difficult to know the exact costs of a negative externality. Nonetheless, this logic may be found within the European Refugee Fund (Betts 2005: 24).

The second instrument, the Coasian property rights, falls back on Robert Coase's idea of assigning property rights for public goods. Without intervention property rights for public goods do not exist, because of the non-excludability criterion. Then, the possibility of trade of the property rights shall be offered. The logic of buying and selling is used in environmental economics. To get pollution under control, the instrument of certificates was introduced. Certificates that permit a certain amount of emission are bought and sold on the stock exchange. As a result, emissions are reduced there where the least costs arise. Obviously, the emissions need to be international public goods, thus, they pollute environment globally. The "logic of 'buying' and 'selling' responsibility" comes closer to the idea of extra-territorial processing (Betts 2005: 22-23). Nevertheless, externalised reception camps are still far away from solutions like tradable emission certificates, because the market would be limited to the EU on one hand and Libya (just to state an example) on the other. Hence, there would be still possible gains of barter by opening the market to others. In addition, Alexander Betts assumes that "high transaction costs and asymmetric bargaining power threaten the theoretical gains in efficiency". Moreover, "it might also allow 'asylum specialisation' by states, allowing them to deal with the claims of groups that are more easily processed or integrated, from an ethnic or linguistic perspective" (Betts 2003: 22-23). The implementation of an external reception camp would not lead to allocative efficiency.

Productive and allocative efficiency by way of illustration

To better understand the results above, they will be illustrated in turn. Let us look at figure 3 to explain the starting situation. At present, the reception of the total amount of asylum seekers is realised within the EU (A). If you read the line from the right (F) to the left (A), you see that the marginal costs (in the sense of net marginal perceived costs as explained in 2.1.3.2) increase with the number of asylum seekers within the EU. The space below the line from the left (A) to the right (F) shows that the marginal benefits increase with each externalised asylum procedure because it is assumed that asylum seekers within the EU are highly associated with political and social costs. Therefore, external EU reception camps are envisaged (from a certain group of people as broadly discussed in Chapter three). The potential host country, to stay with our example, would be Libya as it is one of the top transit countries for asylum seekers on their way to the EU. Its marginal costs and benefits are expressed by the line beginning in the origin. Reading it from the left to the right, it shows the increasing net marginal perceived costs of hosting asylum seekers during their asylum procedures. These political and social costs are supposed to be less perceived in Libya than in the EU. Therefore, the gradient of this line is less than the gradient of the line A to F. If read from the other side (from the right to the left), you may see the marginal benefit for Lybia from avoiding the marginal costs.
Externalised reception camps would signify the processing of a certain amount of asylum seekers (the concerned group is differently defined among the proposals) in Libya which leads to a reallocation of asylum seekers: for example, the asylum seekers from the origin to B are hosted in Libya, the ones from B to F in the EU. A financial compensation (rectangle 0BDC) for Libya is required so that it agrees on such cooperation. In figure 3, it is shown that Libya would do so as long as the financial compensations exceed MC_L. The financial compensation 0BDC minus the costs 0BE leads to benefits 0EDC for Libya. Hence, we suppose that Libya would agree.

However, the aim of such cooperation is the benefit for the EU. The initial allocation raised costs 0AF. Figure 3 shows that the reallocation of asylum seekers by installing extra-territorial processing arises less costs (0BDC) for the financial compensation and BFD for the processing within the EU). As a result, the EU profits from the external solution (ACD). In other words, external reception camps would lead to more productive efficiency because a given output (in this example the processing of the initial

Figure 3:
The financial compensation for Libya
The benefits and costs for Lybia
The benefits and costs for the EU

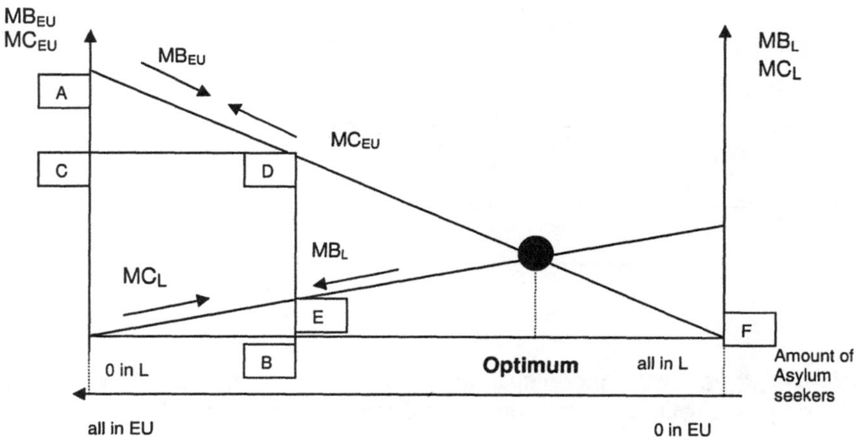

amount of asylum seekers) is reached at lower costs. In this context, externalisation leads to more efficiency because of "burden" sharing.

In contrast, allocative efficiency (Pareto-efficiency) would not be reached. As initially defined, Pareto-efficiency is reached there where a Pareto-improvement is not possible anymore. This is the case where marginal costs equal marginal benefits (the optimum). Our example, the allocation B, is Pareto-inefficient because Pareto-improvement is still possible to the point where a further improvement for the EU is only possible by worsening the situation of Libya (thus to the point where the marginal benefits for the EU do not exceed the marginal costs for Libya anymore). As a result, the economical optimal output (Pareto-efficiency) is reached in H (figure 4) and the EU may maximise its gains to AGH (figure 4). Since the number of externalised asylum procedures can vary depending on the number of spontanous arrivals, the external solution is not an instrument to explicitly reach Pareto-efficiency (except that the optimal allocation could be obtained by coincidence).

Figure 4: Allocative Efficiency

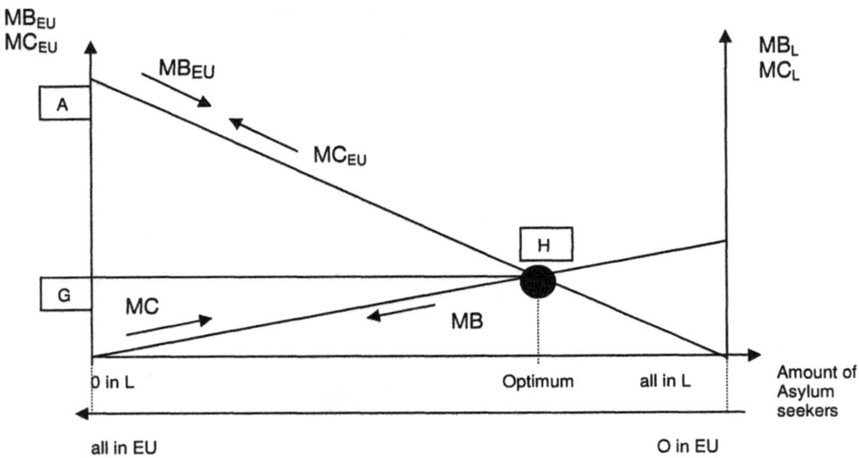

However, these two concepts of efficiency are static models. To complete the analysis of efficiency, the model of dynamic efficiency will be treated in turn.

Dynamic efficiency

Static models imply that several factors that may (or should) change over time are hold constant. In other words, existing levels of certain goods are taken as given. In contrast, the concept of dynamic efficiency adds an inter-temporal dimension to the two static models of productive and allocative efficiency. It may be problematic for global development if the possibility of changing given circumstances is not considered, because innovations in whatever way are not aimed at. That would be especially dangerous in the context of asylum since "the concept of refugees as 'burden' may be changeable over time" (Betts 2005: 26-28). Not considering the dynamic dimension would lead to instructions (from economics to politics) that do not work on changing the image of asylum seekers.

Regarding the influence of politicians and media on the public opinion, this would signify ignorance towards the improvement of the image of asylum seekers. Therefore, the dynamic dimension seems extremely important. Nevertheless, the external solution does not imply an inter-temporal dimension. The aim is not to change the existing circumstances by decreasing the intangible costs within the EU, but to confirm the negative attitudes towards asylum seekers by favouring the deportation of asylum seekers. In other words, more productive efficiency in terms of lower costs could also be obtained by trying to change the perception of the political and social costs over time. This possibility of more efficiency is not considered in the external solution. From this point of view, externalised reception camps are not dynamically efficient.

4.3.3 Externalisation - a more equitable burden sharing system?

To be able to investigate the equity of an externalised solution, different concepts of equity need to be presented. In this context, Robert Pindyck and Daniel Rubinfeld (2001: 576-577) talk about social welfare functions. In economic theory, "social welfare functions" are often used "to describe the particular weights that are applied to each individual's utility in determining what is socially desirable. (...) Each social welfare function can be associated with a particular view about equity". As a result, Pindyck and Rubinfeld distinguish the egalitarian, the Rawlsian, the utilitarian and the market-oriented view of equity. This paper will also use this distinction.

4.3.3.1 The egalitarian view of equity

The egalitarian view of equity requires that every member of a society receives exactly the same amount of goods (Pindyck/Rubinfeld 2001: 577). Used in the context of asylum, the egalitarian view could signify that each country receives the same amount of asylum seekers. But that also implies the non-respect of differences in the population size or in the Gross National Product which would lead to an overburden of small or poor countries. In the case of externalisation, smaller or poorer countries would never agree on such a burden sharing. But there is another interpretation of the egalitarian view which even corresponds more to its initial definition. For each member of a EU country, the country would need to grant asylum to 0.1 asylum seekers. This interpretation is not very realistic since countries like France would never agree on that. They want their expenses for peace keeping missions in conflict regions to be considered.

Another interpretation of the egalitarian view takes the perspective of asylum seekers. In other words, all asylum seekers would need to get the equal amount of goods. As mentioned above, our good of interest is security in the sense of protection. That means that each asylum seeker would receive protection. Regarding the ideas of externalisation and the tightening up of asylum legislation within the EU, this is far from reality. The egalitarian view does not correspond to the asylum policies within the EU at present.

4.3.3.2 The Rawlsian view of equity

This view was founded by the American philosopher John Rawls in his book "The Theory of Justice", published in 1971 (Brockhaus Enzyklopädie 1994: 123). Rawls offers two reasons for the importance of justice. First, it is moral, and second, institutions will be a lot more respected if seen as just. His theory assumes rational individuals that are behind a "veil of ignorance" so that they do not have any information about themselves. They neither know their position in society, nor their historical and geographic origins. Nevertheless, the people are very well informed about social, economical, and psychological facts of the world. Furthermore, Rawls supposes that these individuals meet to discuss the principles of how to distribute goods. Obviously, the negotiators will try to optimise their benefits, but they are not able to estimate them due to the lack of information about themselves. As a result, every rational individual would vote for the improvement of the least well-off persons, because there is the possibility that he or she belongs to them. That is what Rawls calls the "maximin rule" (Barr 1998: 50-51). As a result, "the most equitable allocation" in the sense of Rawls "maximises the utility of the least well-off person in society" (Pindyck/Rubinfeld 2001: 577). Obviously, the criticism of Rawls theory concerns mainly the fact that the veil of ignorance is inexistent and may not be established (Barr 1998: 52).

Regardless whether the veil of ignorance may be established, the externalisation solution does not at all correspond to the Rawlsian view of equity. In a global society, the asylum seekers definitely belong to the least well-off persons. They decide to leave their home countries for different reasons, but with the same aim – a better life in Europe! Thus, if it was about maximising their utility, the EU would need to open their borders instead of closing them. Externalised reception camps with probably little legal control and bad humanitarian circumstances would not contribute to the optimisation of the asylum seeker's utility. In contrast, the external solution strengthens the fortress Europe with the aim not to burden the EU Member States and their citizens. In other words, it aims at more utility for the Europeans instead of the asylum seekers and therefore, externalised reception camps do not establish more equity in the sense of Rawls.

4.3.3.3 The utilitarian view of equity

The term "utilitarianism" comes from the Latin word "utilitas" which means usefulness. The most important representatives are Jeremy Bentham, James Mill and his son John Stuart Mill. Utilitarianism judges measures depending on their contribution to the increase of overall happiness (Brockhaus Enzyklopädie 1994: 15). In other words, equity in the utilitarian sense seeks to "maximise the total utility of all members of society" (Pindyck/Rubinfeld 2001: 577). The term "total utility" may in this context simultaneously be used to "total happiness" or "total welfare" and depends on goods, services, rights, freedom and political power. According to utilitarians, the maximisation of total utility is reached as long as the production and allocation of goods is efficient and the distribution equitable. This will be explained by the following example of "the optimal distribution of income under utilitarianism" (Barr 1998: 48-49). To understand the example better, view figure 5.

We assume that the total income (the line from A to B) needs to be distributed between two individuals, A and B. Their marginal utility is the line aa for A (to read from the left to the right) and bb for B (to read from the right to the left). The marginal utility describes the amount of utility for the individual in the case of an increase in income. These marginal utilities are diminishing, meaning that the utility gain becomes less as the income rises. From a utilitarian point of view, the distribution must be realised by maximising the total welfare. To reach this goal, the distribution needs to be there where the lines aa and bb cut each other. In this first case, the individuals A and B receive exactly the same amount of income. But if their marginal utilities of income are not identical (for example b´b´ instead of bb) the income is distributed unevenly. The possibility of an unjust outcome is broadly criticised. Let us continue with the example. Assuming that the marginal utility of B is represented by the line b´b´ – he enjoys life less because of his serious health problems. Hence, the optimal distribution from a utilitarian perspective would be in point D. In other words, B would get less because of his health problems (Barr 1998: 49). As long as allocative efficiency is reached, even if the ones profiting from it are rich, utilitarians would consider it as justified. As discussed within the examination of efficiency, allocative efficiency and hence, the Pareto criterion, are not fulfilled by the extra-territorial processing.

Figure 5: The optimal distribution of income under utilitarianism
(Barr 1998:49)

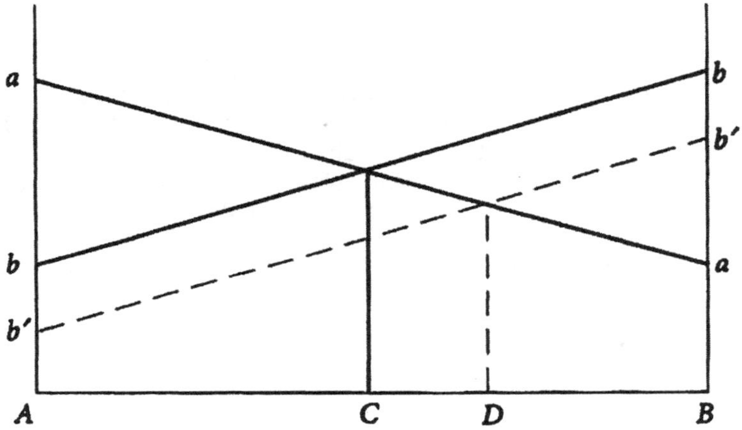

4.3.3.4 The market-oriented view of equity

This view believes in the market and sees the market outcome as the most equitable (Pindyck/Rubinfeld 2001: 577). Therefore, state intervention is not required. This view corresponds to the libertarian theories of society that may be divided in two branches – the 'natural-rights' and the 'empirical' libertarians. The latter are against state intervention because "it will reduce total welfare" and the former are against it for moral reasons (Barr 1998: 45). The market solution matches to the efficiency debate above. However, it does not permit state intervention which is the reason why this view does not go together with the external solution which implies a strong intervention by the EU.

Finally, the Stiglitz and Schönfelder frame would ask for the impact of political decision procedures to look at the feasibility of a project. In this paper, this was already done in 4.2.5 and showed that, from a political point of view, the installation of an external EU reception camp seems quite feasible. However, this chapter did not examine the feasibility of the project, but asked if the external solution contained a more efficient or a more equitable burden sharing system.

4.3.4 Conclusion – more equity or more efficiency?

Within the burden sharing debate, the aim of more efficiency gradually became more important in the last years. Especially the UK proposal of external reception camps demanded it. But if efficiency is aimed at, variety of fixings need to be done to be able to examine external reception camps on its efficiency. These fixings concern the definition of goods, of costs, of the parties profiting from it and of the envisaged concept of efficiency. This was not at all done in the proposals.

The economic qualitative examination above shows that there is only one concept of efficiency that corresponds to the external solution – the productive efficiency. But this is only the case if the above mentioned questions are answered as follows:

- Even if the joint product model is true, the share of publicness (in the sense of public good characteristics) within the goods produced in an asylum system is high. Otherwise, the assumption of market failure (due to the existence of public goods and externalities and with it the legitimation of state intervention would not be given.
- Costs are defined as tangible (financial) and intangible (social and political) costs. Otherwise, if only considering financial costs, the costs would increase and not decrease. Furthermore, as it is strongly assumed in this paper, the costs of spontaneous arrivals (the financial costs plus the social and political costs within the EU) need to exceed the costs of externalisation (processing outside the country plus compensation payments).
- The efficiency aims at the improvement of the EU and not of international society as a whole. The implied intangible costs for asylum seekers are not considered. The profit of the host country of the reception camp (financial compensations higher than their social and political costs) is not envisaged, but is necessary to get their agreement.
- The term efficiency refers to productive efficiency.

These are the conditions under which more productive efficiency is reached and under which the external solution might be seen as a more efficient burden sharing system. But note that the existence of productive efficiency implies a "second-best" solution. The "first-best" solution of a comprehensive efficiency is not reached. In addition, an efficient outcome "may lead to great inequalities" (Samuelson/Nordhaus 1995: 33). The examination of externalisation contributing to more equity did not result in any positive answers. More equity on a global scale would not be reached by externalising asylum procedures. In contrast, especially condition number 3 supposes that the improvement of the EU is the aim. On a global scale, global equity in the sharing of the asylum burden is rather decreased.

To conclude, the economic qualitative analysis shows that the external solution would more likely correspond to a more efficient model rather than to a more equitable burden sharing system. This result seems to be important for everybody to know which aim would be reached if he or she agrees on such a measure. The decision for one aim or the other is not commented in this chapter and is purely ideological. Nevertheless, the author of this paper wants to emphasise that the analysis in this chapter tries to be a neutral and economic examination to be able to answer the research question. It does not consider moral reservations about the connection of the institution of asylum to efficiency (even if they exist).

5 Conclusions

Causes

The burden sharing debate is revived as soon as some nation states estimate their contribution to the provision of a certain international public good like protection/security as disproportionate. Such estimation always depends on the relation between the contribution and other numbers like the population size, the GDP, and/or the unemployment rate. Depending on how being "overburdened" is defined, some countries are advantaged, others are disadvantaged. Densely populated countries for example would need to contribute more to the asylum system, if the burden was defined in relation to the population size.

Obviously, some nation states try to influence the burden sharing debate in a way that they are advantaged. Therefore, the objective of "burden-sharing instead of burden-shifting" is formulated. Within this debate, a variety of instruments heading either towards a more equitable or a more efficient burden-sharing system exist. The former is said to be reached by policy harmonisation or quota settings, while the latter is assumed to be obtained by the incorporation of a market mechanism. The inclusion of "trade" within the asylum field would signify physical transfer of asylum seekers which is not required in the case of policy harmonisation and quota settings.

In the recent years, the EU has been working on a Common EU Asylum System to share the burden among their Member States. But more and more EU Member States have wanted to reduce their asylum burden, especially because the perceived social and political costs associated with asylum seekers were gradually increasing. In such a situation, the construction of a Common EU Asylum System faces some difficulties as it is shown by the protracted procedure of agreeing on minimum standards for asylum seekers. Within this development, in spring 2003, the UK proposed extra-territorial processing for asylum seekers in reception camps outside the EU. Certain categories of spontaneous arrivals would be sent there to have their claims processed. If granted asylum, they would be received by a certain EU member state. If not, they would be sent back to their regions of origin. The UNHCR stated a counter-proposal that foresees such reception camps within the EU, but at the borders of it. In summer 2004, when another refugee drama happened in the Mediterranean Sea, Otto Schily, the German Home Minister, offered the external solution. A year later, in September 2005, he recalled people's attention to it. Even if in the case of the UK, the UNHCR, and Otto Schily, the reasons given for formulating the idea of externalised EU reception camps were different, this paper places the externalisation idea into the burden sharing debate. It may be interpreted as an instrument that foresees physical transfer of asylum seekers and that incorporates a "trade" element. In other words, the EU would rent territory in a state outside the EU to realise the asylum processing there.

Potential consequences

This paper asked about the adequacy of an externalised EU reception camp as a burden sharing instrument. To be able to answer this question, the potential consequences in case of realising external EU reception camps are examined on the basis of different methods of analysis. First, the analysis of newspaper articles and organisation statements show that the majority of the EU Member States support such an external solution, while the majority of organisations oppose it.

Second, the adequacy of externalisation itself is investigated from a legal, humanitarian and political point of view. The results: it is inadequate because it would contradict international law. Even if it may be interpreted that neither the Universal Declaration of Human Rights (Art. 14.1) nor the 1951 Geneva Convention (Art. 1) demands protection for persecuted people on the soil of the concerned nation state, it is definitely only allowed in safe countries. It is highly doubtful if states like Libya or the Ukraine would be 'safe' for asylum seekers. However, even if the processing on other territory was lawful, the transfer of responsibility for asylum seekers to other states is illegal. Moreover, discrimination, detention, and inhuman treatment are forbidden in several international laws, but very likely to occur in such externalised reception camps. That goes together with the humanitarian perspective and shows that externalisation would not be compatible with the humanitarian principle.

Furthermore, the elaboration of the proposals is not satisfactory since former evaluations are not considered, potential risks of, for example, forced transfer and unrealistic components like open reception camps are not presented. Based on the legal and humanitarian consequences and on the unsatisfactory elaboration of the proposals, the external solution may be estimated as inadequate.

In contrast, the examination shows that externalisation may be estimated as politically usable, because the majority of EU citizens want less liberal asylum policies. In other words, a political party could decide to favour the externalisation of asylum procedures, because it could lead to the increase of votes. Therefore, the external solution is adequate in terms of its political usability.

In a third step, the externalisation is looked at in its function as a burden-sharing instrument. It is examined whether it is an instrument that would lead towards a more efficient or a more equitable burden sharing system. A variety of concepts of efficiency and of equity were introduced to finally come to the following results: externalisation would not lead to more equity, but it is an instrument that leads – under certain circumstances (reproduced in the conclusion of Chapter 4.3) – to more efficiency. In other words, the burden of asylum would be split between the EU and another country (in our example Libya) in a way that finally the outcome is productively more efficient. Since the political and social costs of asylum seekers are assumed to be higher in the EU than in Libya, the EU would pay Libya for offering territory where the asylum processing would be realised. As a result, the EU would not have to bare its high political and social costs anymore and would therefore be able to profit from the external solution.

Synthesising the results

We could summarise the results of this paper as follows: externalised EU reception camps would be inadequate from a legal and humanitarian point of view, but adequate in terms of its political usability and – under certain circumstances – its economic efficiency. To finally be able to answer the question whether it is an adequate EU refugee burden sharing instrument, a normative assessment needs to be done. After the very subjective decision for how weighing the different perspectives, the external solution can be estimated to be an adequate or an inadequate instrument.

To conclude, I would like to reveal my own "normative assessment" that will show why I estimate the external solution to be inadequate. I strongly believe that a society profits from the emphasis on the humanitarian perspective when taking decisions. Therefore, the humanitarian consequences of a measure taken should be valued the highest. This belief already shows why externalisation is in my opinion inadequate. Furthermore, the aim of economic efficiency may be important, especially if it is about motivating countries to contribute to a common burden sharing system. But if the contribution to an efficient burden sharing system signifies the breach of the humanitarian principle, then heading towards more efficiency is in my opinion no longer justified. It is the same with the political usability of a measure. High political usability of externalisation may explain why some people support it. But politicians should not justify inhuman measures on the basis of the will of the people. In contrast, politicians and media should use their power to broaden people's horizon. For these reasons, I estimate externalised EU reception camps to be inadequate. If more security for asylum seekers was really the aim, as argued in Chapter 4.2, they should be offered legal immigration possibilities.

Impulse for further research

This paper is based on a variety of assumptions. Especially interesting is the assumption (confirmed by a variety of experts) that asylum seekers would continue to try to arrive illegally to the EU instead of voluntarily going to EU reception camps. It would be highly remarkable to give empirical evidence for the truth of this assumption. As a result, it could be shown that the whole externalisation idea would not succeed in an attempt to contribute to more security for asylum seekers. Empirical evidence could be won out of qualitative interviews with asylum seekers in Northern African states. Such qualitative research exceeded the capacities of this paper, but is highly recommended for a further research project.

Bibliography

- **Amnesty International (1996)** "Southeast Asia: Other governments should follow Philippines government new stance on treatment failed by asylum seekers", *AI Index: ASA 03/001/1996*, News Service 29/96, 16 February 1996, available at: http://web.amnesty.org/library/Index/ENGASA030011996?open&of=ENG-PHL [accessed 28 April 2005].
- **Amnesty International (2002)** "Australia-Pacific: Offending human dignity – the Pacific solution", *AI Index: ASA 12/009/2002*, 26 August 2002, available at: http://web.amnesty.org/library/Index/ENGASA120092002?open&of=ENG-NRU [accessed 29 March 2005].
- **Amnesty International (2003)** UK/EU/UNHCR: Unlawful and Unworkable – Amnesty International's view on proposals for extra-territorial processing of asylum claims, *AI Index: IOR 61/004/2003*, available at: http://web.amnesty.org/library/pdf/IOR610042003ENGLISH/$File/IOR6100403.pdf [accessed 10 March 2005].
- **Barbou des Places, Ségolène / Deffains, Bruno (2003)** "Cooperation in the shadow of regulatory competition : the case of asylum legislation in Europe", *International Review of Law and Economics*, vol. 23, issue 4, 2003.
- **Barnett, Laura (2002)** "Global Governance and the evolution of international refugee regime", *UNHCR Working Paper No. 54*, February 2002, available at: http://www.unhcr.ch/cgibin/texis/vtx/home/opendoc.pdf?tbl=RESEARCH&id=3c7529495&page=research [accessed 3 May 2005].
- **Barr, Nicholas (1998)** *"The Economics of the Welfare State",* Third Edition, Oxford University Press, Oxford 1998.
- **BBC (2002)** "Q&A: Australia's 'Pacific Solution'", *BBC News online*, 5 February 2002, available at: http://news.bbc.co.uk/1/hi/world/asia-pacific/1802364.stm [accessed 29 March 2005].
- **Betts, Alexander (2003)** "The political economy of extra-territorial processing: separating 'purchaser" from 'provider' state", UNHCR *Working Paper No. 91*, June 2003, available at: http://www.reliefweb.int/library/RSC_Oxford/data/UNHCR%20Working%20Papers/91%20extra-territorial%20processing.pdf [accessed 9 May 2005].
- **Betts, Alexander (2004)** "The International Relations of the "New" Extraterritorial Approaches to Refugee Protection: Explaining the Policy Initiatives of the Uk Government and UNHCR", *Refuge*, Vol.22, Nr. 1, May

2004, available at:
http://www.yorku.ca/crs/Refuge/Abstracts%20and%20Articles/Vol%2022%20No%201/betts.pdf [accessed 17 September 2005].
▪ **Betts, Alexander (2005)** "What does 'Efficiency' mean in the Context of the Global Refugee Regime?", Centre on Migration, Policy and Society, *Working Paper No. 9*, University of Oxford 2005, available at:
http://www.compas.ox.ac.uk/publications/papers/WP0509.pdf [accessed 10 May 2005].
▪ **Blair, Tony (2003)** "Letter to Costas Simitis", London 10 March 2003, available at:
http://www.statewatch.org/news/2003/apr/blair-simitis-asile.pdf [accessed 19 March 2005].
▪ **Boyer, Mark A. (1989)** "Trading Public Goods in the Western Alliance System", *Journal of Conflict Resolution*, Vol.33, No.4, Sage Publications Inc., London December 1989.
▪ **Brockhaus Enzyklopädie (1994)** "Rawls, John",19th Edition, Volume 18, F.A. Brockhaus, Mannheim 1994.
▪ **Brockhaus Enzyklopädie (1994)** "Utilitarismus",19th Edition, Volume 23, F.A. Brockhaus, Mannheim 1994.
▪ **Czaika, Mathias (2005)** "A Refugee Burden Index: methodology and its application", *Working paper*, Oxford Brookes University, 13 – 14 May 2005.
▪ **Catz, Petra / Edminster, Steve / Frelick, Bill / Loescher, Gil / Milner, James (2003)** "Responding to the Asylum and Access Challenge. An agenda for comprehensive engagement in protected refugee situations ", U.S. Committee for Refugees (USCR) and European Council on Refugees and Exiles (ECRE), April 2003, available at:
http://www.ecre.org/publications/gmf.pdf [accessed 14 April 2005].
▪ **Churches Committee for Migrants in Europe (2004)** "Against the creation of camps at European borders", *appeal* of 12 October 2004, available at:
http://www.meltingpot.org/articolo3888.html [accessed 24 February 2005].
▪ **Commission of the European Communities (2003**) "Towards more accessible, equitable and managed asylum systems", *Communication from the Commission to the Council and the European Parliament*, COM (2003) 315 final, Brussels 3 June 2003, available at:
http://www.ecre.org/eu_developments/debates/comukcomm.pdf [accessed 1 March 2005].
▪ **Commission of the European Communities (2005)** "On regional protection programmes", *Communication from the Commission to the Council and the European Parliament*, COM (2005) 388 final, Brussels 1 September 2005, available at:

http://europa.eu.int/eurlex/lex/LexUriServ/site/en/com/2005/com2005_0388en01.pdf [accessed 12 September 2005].

- **Council of Europe (1950)** *"European Convention on Human Rights",* Rome 4 November 1950, available at: http://www.hri.org/docs/ECHR50.html#C.Art3 [accessed 22 March 2005].
- **Daniel, Tobias (2004)** "EU will Auffanglager testen", *Europa Digital* 4 October 2004, available at: www.europa-digital.de [accessed 17 December 2004].
- **Dietrich, Stefan (2004)**: „Schily und die Pharisäer", FAZ-commentary, *Frankfurter Allgemeine Zeitung*, print version, 24 July 2004, nr. 170, page 1.
- **ECRE (2003)** "Statement of the European Council on Refugees and Exiles on the European Council Meeting on the 21st and 22nd March 2003", *Press Release*, 17 March 2003, available at: http://www.ecre.org/statements/Council%20March%202003.shtml [accessed 19 March 2005].
- **European Council (March 2003)** "*Presidency Conclusions on the Brussels European Council on the 20th and 21st March 2003*", 8410/03, Brussels 5 May 2003, available at: http://ue.eu.int/ueDocs/cms_Data/docs/pressData/en/ec/75136.pdf [accessed 19 March 2005].
- **European Union (2000)** "Charter of Fundamental Rights of the European Union", *Official Journal of the European Communities*, C 364/1, 18 December 2000, available at: http://www.europarl.eu.int/charter/pdf/text_en.pdf [accessed 22 March 2005].
- **Fagerlund, Jessica / Liebaut, Fabrice / Noll, Gregor (2002)** "Study on the feasibility of processing asylum claims outside the EU against the background of the Common European Asylum System and the goal of a common asylum procedure", *final report* , Danish Human Rights Centre, 2002, available at: http://europa.eu.int/comm/justice_home/doc_centre/asylum/common/asylumstudy_dchr_2002_en.pdf [accessed 5 February 2005].
- **Finch, Nadine / Mac Donald, Ian (2003)** "Opinion on the UK proposal", *Justice* 22 June 2003, available at: http://www.justice.org.uk/images/pdfs/asylumprocessingopinion.pdf [accessed 21 March 2005].
- **Frankfurter Allgemeine Sonntagszeitung (25 July 2004)** „Beckstein stimmt Schily zu", *Frankfurter Allgemeine Sonntagszeitung*, 25 July 2004, nr. 30, available at: http://www.faz.net/s/Rub28FC768942F34C5B8297CC6E16FFC8B4/Doc~E1EA008431C7E4F348FACE66523F9F272~ATpl~Ecommon~Scontent.html#top [accessed 12 December 2004].

- **Frey, Bruno S. (1997)** *"Not just for the money. An economic theory of Personal Motivation"*, Edward Elgar Publishing, Cheltenham UK 1997.
- **Frey, Bruno S. (2001)** *"Inspiring Economics. Human Motivation in Political Economy"*, Edward Elgar Publishing, Cheltenham UK 2001.
- **Gibney, Matthew J. (2002)** "Security and the ethics of asylum after 11 September", *Forced Migration Review*, vol. 13, Refugee Studies Centre June 2002, available at: http://www.fmreview.org/FMRpdfs/FMR13/fmr13full.pdf [accessed 14 September 2005].
- **Gibney, Matthew J. (2004)** *"The Ethics and Politics of Asylum. Liberal Democracy and the Response to Refugees"*, Cambridge University Press, Cambridge 2004.
- **Hartley, Keith / Sandler, Todd (2001)** "Economics of Alliances: The Lessons for Collective Action", *Journal of Economic Literature*, Vol. 39, September 2001, pp. 869 – 896.
- **Hatton, Timothy J. (2004)** "Seeking asylum in Europe", in: *Economic Policy*, nr. 38, Blackwell Publishing Ltd, UK April 2004.
- **Hiscock, Stéphane (2002)** "Nauru and the Pacific Solution", January – February 2002, *The Courier ACP-EU*, available at: http://europa.eu.int/comm./development/body/publications/courier/courier190/en/en_021.pdf [accessed 29 March 2005].
- **House of Lords (2004)** "Handling EU asylum claims: new approaches examined", European Union Committee, *11th Report of Session 2003-04*, HL Paper 74, published by the Authority of the House of Lords 30 April 2004, available at: http://www.publications.parliament.uk/pa/ld200304/ldselect/ldeucom/74/74.pdf [accessed 8 March 2005].
- **House of Lords (2005)** "The Hague Programme: a five year agenda for EU justice and home affairs", European Union Committee, *10th Report of Session 2004-05,* HL Paper 84, published by the Authority of the House of Lords 23 March 2005, available at: http://www.statewatch.org/news/2005/mar/hol-hague-programme.pdf [accessed 30 March 2005].
- **Human Rights Watch (2002)** "By invitation only. Australian Asylum Policy", *Human Rights Watch* Vol. 14, No. 10 (C), December 2002, available at: http://hrw.org/reports/2002/australia/australia1202.pdf [accessed 29 March 2005].
- **Kingston, Margo (2002)** "Terror, boat people, and getting old", *The Sidney Morning Herald* 15 May 2002, available at: http://www.smh.com.au/articles/2002/05/15/1021415009323.html [accessed 20 April 2005].

- **Kopp, Karl (2004)** "Deutsch-Österreichische Arbeitsteilung: Demontage des europäischen Asylrechts", *press release*, Pro Asyl 22 September 2004, available at: http://www.proasyl.de/presse04/sep22.htm [accessed 17 December 2004].
- **Kreickenbaum, Martin (2004)**: „Erstes Flüchtlingslager der EU soll schon bald in Libyen entstehen", 24 August 2004, available at: www.wsws.org/de/2004/asyl-a24.shtml [accessed 12 December 2004].
- **Macdonald Sarah (2002)** "Australia's Pacific Solution", *report for Correspondent BBC News*, 26 September 2002, available at: http://news.bbc.co.uk/1/hi/programmes/correspondent/2279330.stm [accessed 29 March 2005].
- **Mankiw, Gregory N. (2001)** *"Principles of Economics"*, Second Edition, Harcourt College Publishers, New York et al. 2001.
- **Milner, James (2000)** "Sharing the Security Burden: Towards the Convergence of Refugee Protection and State Security", Refugee Studies Centre, *Working Paper* No. 4, Queen Elizabeth House, University of Oxford May 2000, available at: http://www.rsc.ox.ac.uk/PDFs/workingpaper4.pdf [accessed 04 May 2005].
- **Miraglia, Filippo (2005)** "Les interceptions maritimes", *Study and mobilisation days*, Sevilla 20 – 21 June 2005, available at: http://www.migreurop.org/article852.html [accessed 9 September 2005].
- **Newland, Kathleen (1995)** "The Impact of U.S. Refugee Policies on U.S. Foreign Policy: A Case of Tail Wagging the Dog?", available at: Teitelbaum, Michael S. / Weiner, Myron (1995) "*Threatened Peoples, Threatened Borders: World Migration and U.S. Policy*", The American Assembly, New York 1995.
- **Noll, Gregor (2003)** "Visions of the Exceptional: Legal and Theoretical Issues Raised by Transit Processing Centres and Protection Zones", *working paper*, Faculty of Law, Lund University Sweden 2003, available at: http://www.ecre.org/eu_developments/debates/noll_response_rev.pdf [accessed 23 March 2005].
- **Prasad, Raekha (2003)** "Refugee camps don't work", *The Guardian* 10 February 2003, available at: http://www.guardian.co.uk/print/0,3858,4602248-103677,00.html [accessed 21 March 2005].
- **Pindyck, Robert S. / Rubinfeld, Daniel L. (2001)** „*Microeconomics*", Fifth Edition, Prentice Hall International, London et al. 2001.
- **Quah, Euston / Tan K.C. (1998)** „The siting problem of NIMBY facilities: cost-benefit analysis and auction mechanisms", *Environment and Planning: Government and Policy C*, vol.16, 1998, Pion Limited, London 1998.

- **Samuelson, Paul A. / Nordhaus, William D. (1995)** *"Economics"*, 15th Edition, McGraw-Hill Inc., New York et al. 1995.
- **Schily Otto (2005)** "Effektiver Schutz für Flüchtlinge, wirkungsvolle Bekämpfung illegaler Migration – Überlegungen des Bundesministers des Innern zur Errichtung einer EU-Aufnahmeeinrichtung in Nordafrika", *press conference* 9 september 2005, available at: http://www.bmi.bund.de/Internet/Content/Nachrichten/Pressemitteilungen/2005/09/Fluechtlingsschutz.html [accessed 13 September 2005].
- **Schuck, Peter H. (1997)** "Refugee Burden-Sharing: A Modest Proposal", *Yale Journal of International Law*, Vol. 22, No.2, Summer 1997.
- **Schumpeter, Joseph A.(1955)** "*Kapitalismus, Sozialismus und Demokratie*", Francke, Bern 1955 (engl. 1942).
- **Statewatch (March 2003)** "Asylum in the EU: the beginning of the end?", March 2003, available at: http://www.statewatch.org/news/2003/mar/25asylum.htm [accessed 13 March 2005].
- **Statewatch (June 2003)** "EU buffer states and UNHCR "processing" centres and "safe havens", June 2003, available at: http://www.statewatch.org/news/2003/jun/07eubuffer.htm [accessed 13 March 2005].
- **Stiglitz Joseph E. / Bruno Schönfelder (1989)** "Finanzwissenschaft", 2nd Edition, Internationale Standardlehrbücher der Wirtschafts- und Sozialwissenschaften, R. Oldenbourg Verlag, München Wien 1989.
- **Suhrke, Astri (1998)** "Burden-sharing during Refugee Emergencies: The Logic of Collective versus National Action", *Journal of Refugee Studies*, Vol. 11, No. 4, 1998.
- **Thielemann, Eiko (2003)** „Does Policy Matter? On Governments' Attempts to Control Unwanted Migration", *European Institute Working Paper*, May 2003, available at: http://www.lse.ac.uk/collections/europeaninstitute/pdfs/Eiworkingpaper2003-02.pdf [accessed 05 May 2005].
- **Thielemann, Eiko (2005)** "Towards Refugee Burden-Sharing in the European Union. State Interests and Policy Options.", *Conference paper*, prepared for the Ninth Biennial International Conference on the European Union Studies Association (USA), 31 March – 2 April 2005, Austin, Texas, available at: http://aei.pitt.edu/archive/00003001/01/Thielemann-EUSA-Austin-2005.txt [accessed 12 May 2005].
- **Tietenberg, Tom (2003)** *"Environmental and Natural Resource economics"*, Sixth Edition, Addison Wesley Edition, Boston et al. 2003.
- **Travis, Alan (2003)** "Amnesty condemns 'safe haven' scheme", *The Guardian* 28 March 2003, available at:

http://www.guardian.co.uk/uk_news/story/0,,924339,00.html [accessed 10 March 2005].

- **United Nations General Assembly (1948)** *"Universal Declaration of Human Rights"*, Adopted and proclaimed by General Assembly resolution 217 A (III) of 10 December 1948, available at: http://www.un.org/Overview/rights.html [accessed 22 March 2005]
- **UNHCR (1996)** "*Convention and Protocol. Relating to the status of refugees"*, Geneva March 1996, available at: http://www.asylumsupport.info/publications/unhcr/convention.pdf [accessed 12 February 2005].
- **UNHCR (March 2003)** "UNHCR working proposal", *UNHCR working paper*, March 2003, available at: http://www.statewatch.org/news/2003/jun/unhcr.pdf [accessed 10 March 2005].
- **UNHCR (April 2003a)** "Explanation of the regional prong", *UNHCR working paper*, April 2003, available at: http://www.statewatch.org/news/2003/jun/unhcr.pdf [accessed 10 March 2005].
- **UNHCR (April 2003b)** "Explanation of the EU-prong", *UNHCR working paper*, April 2003, available at: http://www.statewatch.org/news/2003/jun/unhcr.pdf [accessed 10 March 2005].
- **UNHCR (June 2003)** "UNHCR's three-pronged proposal", *UNHCR working paper*, Geneva June 2003, available at: http://www.ecre.org/eu_developments/debates/unhcr3prong.DOC [accessed 10 March 2005].
- **UNHCR (December 2003)** "A revised 'EU-prong' proposal", *UNHCR working paper*, Geneva 22 December 2003, available at: House of Lords (2004) "Handling EU asylum claims: new approaches examined", European Union Committee, 11th Report of Session 2003-04, HL Paper 74, Appendix 7, published by the Authority of the House of Lords 30 April 2004, available at: http://www.publications.parliament.uk/pa/ld200304/ldselect/ldeucom/74/74.pdf [accessed 8 March 2004].
- **UNHCR (2005)** „Asylum Levels and Trends in Industrialized Countries. Overview of asylum applications lodged in Europe and non-European industrialized countries in 2004", Population data unit, Division of operational support, 1 March 2005, available at: http://www.unhcr.ch/cgibin/texis/vtx/statistics/opendoc.pdf?tbl=STATISTICS&id=422439144 [accessed 15 March 2005].
- **US Navy (2002)** "Guantanamo Bay – a brief history", 18 January 2002, available at:

http://www.nsgtmo.navy.mil/gazette/History_98-64/Brief%20History.htm [accessed 29 March 2005].
- **US Navy (2005)** "The history of the USNS Comfort", available at: http://www.comfort.navy.mil/facts.html [accessed 29 March 2005].
- **Van Gorp, Baldwin (2001)** "The Implementation of the Asylum Policy: Which Frame Dominates the Debate?", *Workshop paper*, Discourse & Institutional Reforms, ECPR 29th Session, Grenoble, 6-11 April 2001.
- **Varian, Hal R. (2001)** *"Grundzüge der Mikroökonomik"*, Fifth Edition, Olsenbourg Wissenschaftsverlag, München 2001.
- **Viusa, Nicole (2004)** "Schily erhält EU-Zuspruch für Auffangzentren", Pro Asyl 1 October 2004, available at: http://www.proasyl.de/pipermail/migration-hh/2004-October/000066.html [accessed 17 December 2004].
- **Wälterlin, Urs (2005)** „Australierin aus eigenem Land abgeschoben", *Der Standard* 04 May 2005.
- **Zeiske, Kathrin (2005)** "In Erwartung der ‚sicheren Wiederbeheimatung'. Die Situation von MigrantInnen in den Abschiebungsgefängnissen von Mexiko und Guatemala.", available at: http://www.ila-bonn.de/artikel/ila283/abschiebung.htm [accessed 07 April 2005].

List of Figures

List of Acronyms

CDU	Christlich Demokratische Union
CSU	Christlich Soziale Union
ECHR	European Convention on Human Rights
ECtHR	European Court of Human Rights
ECRE	European Council on Refugees and Exiles
ERF	European Refugee Fund
EU	European Union
FAZ	Frankfurter Allgemeine Zeitung
GDP	Gross Domestic Product
ICAR	Information Centre about Asylum and Refugees in the UK
IGC	Intergovernmental Conference
IGC	Intergovernmental Consultations on Asylum, Refugees and Migration Policies in Europe, North America and Australia
ILPA	Immigration Law Practitioners' Association
IOM	International Organisation of Migration
IRO	International Refugee Organisation
JHA	Justice and Home Affairs
NG0	Non Governmental Organisation
NIMBY	Not In My Backyard
OECD	Organisation for Economic Cooperation and Development
PEP	Protected Entry Procedures
PZ	Protection Zone
RPA	Regional Protection Area
RPC	Regional Protection Centre
SPD	Sozialdemokratische Partei Deutschlands
TPC	Transit Processing Centre
UDHR	Universal Declaration on Human Rights
UNHCR	United Nations High Commissioner for Refugees
USCR	United States Committee for Refugees

Peter Lang · Europäischer Verlag der Wissenschaften

Bernd von Hoffmann (ed.)

Towards a Common European Immigration Policy

Reports and Discussions of a Symposium held in Trier on October 24th and 25th, 2002

Frankfurt am Main, Berlin, Bern, Bruxelles, New York, Oxford, Wien, 2003.
279 pp., num. fig., num. tab.
Legal Policy Symposium. Edited in the Institute for Legal Policy at the University of Trier by Bernd von Hoffmann and Gerhard Robbers. Vol. 1
ISBN 978-3-631-51296-8 · pb. € 45.–*

Immigration policy has become a very controversial subject for legal policy discussion in the European Union. Dramatic demographic changes make it evident that immigration is one of the means for replacing an ageing labour force and maintaining the social system. A comprehensive immigration policy has to take into account the needs of the labour market, efficient selection procedures and the cost of integration. In October 2002 the Institute for Legal Policy at the University of Trier held a workshop on those issues. Eminent specialists from different European countries presented papers on different aspects of immigration and integration in an interdisciplinary way. These papers and the discussion reports are contained in this volume.

Contents: *Rainer Münz:* Migration and Demographic Change in Europe · *Karin Oellers-Frahm*: National Immigration Policies in Comparative Perspective · *Felicita Medved:* A Common European Immigration Policy or How Common is Common Enough?· *Christian Calliess:* The Constitutional Framework of a Common European Immigration Policy · *Anastasios Bisopoulos:* Immigration and Labour Market Policies in the European Union · *Joanna Apap:* Shaping Europe's Migration Policy: A Comparative Analysis of Member States' "Green Card" Legislation · *Heinz Werner:* The Integration of Foreign Workers into the Labour Market: An EU Perspective · *Sandrine van der Velde*: Three Paradoxes in the Community Right to Family Reunification for Migrant Workers · and more

Frankfurt am Main · Berlin · Bern · Bruxelles · New York · Oxford · Wien
Distribution: Verlag Peter Lang AG
Moosstr. 1, CH-2542 Pieterlen
Telefax 0041 (0) 32 / 376 17 27

*The €-price includes German tax rate
Prices are subject to change without notice

Homepage http://www.peterlang.de

Kolibri 360 GmbH
Ferdinand-Jühlke-Straße 7
99095 Erfurt, Deutschland
produktsicherheit@kolibri360.de